ARAB RELATIONS IN THE MIDDLE EAST

MIDEAST AFFAIRS SERIES

1. Arab Relations in the Middle East
   The Road to Realignment

ARAB RELATIONS IN THE MIDDLE EAST

The Road to Realignment

Edited by
COLIN LEGUM and HAIM SHAKED

The Shiloah Center
for Middle Eastern and African Studies
Tel Aviv University

HM
HOLMES & MEIER PUBLISHERS, INC.
New York and London

First published in the United States of America 1979 by
Holmes & Meier Publishers, Inc.
30 Irving Place
New York, N.Y. 10003

Great Britain:
Holmes & Meier Publishers, Ltd
Hillview House
1, Hallswelle Parade
Finchley Road
London NW11 ODL

LIBRARY OF CONGRESS CATALOGING
IN PUBLICATION DATA

Main entry under title:

Arab relations in the Middle East.

(Mideast affairs series; I)
Essays first appeared in the Middle East contemporary survey.

I. Arab countries—Politics and government—Addresses, essays, lectures. II. Jewish-Arab relations—1973—Addresses, essays, lectures.
I. Legum, Colin, II. Shaked, Haim. III. Mekhon Shiloaḥ le-ḥeḳer ha-Mizraḥ ha-tikhon ṿe-Afriḳaḥ. IV. Series.
DF63.1.A68 1978   320.9'17'4927   78-20888

ISBN 0-8419-0447-2

Manufactured in the United States of America

Contents

Note

For references to articles mentioned in the body of the text, readers are referred to Volume 1 of *Middle East Contemporary Survey* (New York and London, 1978).

Preface

Arab Relations in the Middle East is the first of a series of volumes exploring current affairs in the Middle East. The essays in this volume first appeared in the *Middle East Contemporary Survey* (MECS), which has recently been published. The purpose of this new series is to reach a wider audience of readers interested in Middle Eastern affairs than is likely to be reached by the comprehensive MECS. While each volume in this new series is planned to stand on its own, readers will nevertheless benefit from reading them alongside each other and, especially, in conjunction with MECS, which reviews every country in the Middle East as well as treating all the major issues raised by the conflicts and relationships in the region.

Of the three dimensions in the Middle Eastern conflict—Arab/Israel, International, and Inter-Arab—it is usual to pay more attention to the first two than to the third; yet, in the long run, Inter-Arab relations are bound to be the most decisive factor in determining both the future of Arab/Israeli relations and the extent of international involvement in the Middle East.

This view is substantially borne out by the serious tensions experienced in the Arab world in the period leading up to the historic Camp David agreement and, especially, by its repercussions. This particular volume covers the crucial period immediately before the Camp David summit. It begins with the important Riyadh conference in October 1976 and ends with the realignment of Arab states and forces following President Sadat's dramatic visit to Jerusalem in November 1977. The essays examine relations between the Arab states; the internal and external relations of the Palestine Liberation Organization (PLO) and other Palestinian groups; the workings of the Arab League; and developments on the West Bank and in the Gaza Strip. A concluding section provides an extensive chronology and commentary on political developments in the Arab/Israeli conflict.

All the contributions in this volume are by members of the academic staff of the Shiloah Center of Middle Eastern Studies at Tel Aviv University.

Colin Legum, Editor
Haim Shaked, Academic Editor
Middle East Contemporary Survey

Inter-Arab Relations

DANIEL DISHON

With the assistance of VARDA BEN-ZVI

THE RIYADH CONFERENCE: A WATERSHED

The conference held in Riyadh from 16-18 October 1976 ended one period in inter-Arab relations and ushered in another. This important meeting was attended by Saudi Arabia's King Khālid, the Presidents of Egypt, Syria and Lebanon, the ruler of Kuwait, and the PLO chairman Yāsir 'Arafāt. The pre-Riyadh constellation had clustered around the events generated by the second Sinai Agreement of 1 September 1975. These were characterized: 1) by the increasingly vocal, increasingly strident Syrian-Egyptian dispute for which the Sinai Agreement provided the backdrop, but the roots of which actually went back to the war of October 1973; 2) by the energetic attempt on the part of Syria to carve out for itself an area of exclusive, or at least predominant, influence in Jordan and Lebanon and ascendancy over the PLO (and thus, possibly, over a future Palestinian state); 3) by the inter-Arab reverberations of the civil war in Lebanon and, from June 1976 onwards, of Syria's massive military intervention there; 4) by a vigorous, but eventually unsuccessful, campaign on the part of Iraq and Libya designed to establish a radical bloc of "rejectionist" states by drawing Syria into a combination with themselves, Algeria and the PLO.

All this time, Egypt had been on the defensive and had come to be increasingly isolated in the Arab world. In the Syrian-Egyptian quarrel, Saudi Arabia—its weight in inter-Arab relations steadily on the rise ever since the early 1970s—had at first inclined towards Syria to an almost imperceptible degree, then equally slightly towards Egypt. From the early summer of 1976 onwards, its main endeavour had been to reconcile Syria and Egypt and to re-establish the Syrian-Egyptian-Saudi triangle that had prepared and conducted the 1973 war. It was Saudi urging (seconded by Kuwait) that brought about the Riyadh conference.

Saudi prompting would not of itself have been sufficient, however, had not the overall situation in the Arab world been ripe for realignment. The Syrian army by now held positions commanding the approaches to Beirut, Tripoli and Sidon. The Syrian leadership realized that it had more to gain from completing the occupation of Lebanon with the blessing of the Arab states than against the combined pressures of all of them (with only Jordan loyal to the Syrian line in Lebanon). In a situation in which neither outside Arab states, nor the PLO and their anti-Syrian Lebanese allies, were any longer capable of stopping the completion of the Syrian military moves, the political price Syria would have to pay for Arab sanction would no longer be too onerous. It would be outweighed by the military advantage of not having to fight for the major towns, and by the domestic gains likely to follow a cessation of Syrian armed action against Lebanese Muslims and the PLO. (For the domestic repercussions of Syria's intervention in Lebanon, see survey of Syria.)

Egypt, for her part, realized at this juncture that its approval of Syria's exclusive position in Lebanon could still be traded off for a Syrian undertaking to call off the anti-Egyptian propaganda war. Also, a reconciliation at this point would allow the Egyptians to claim credit later for having saved the PLO from being crushed altogether, and ʻArafāt from being forced out of the PLO leadership by Syria. Saudi Arabia expected—correctly, as it turned out—that its initiative in ending the Lebanese war and the Syrian-Egyptian dispute at one stroke, together with the venue of the conference in Riyadh and King Khālid's chairmanship of it, would enchance its image as arbiter of all-Arab affairs.

Over and above these considerations, all three leaders had become preoccupied with the approach of the US presidential election, realizing that it would be advantageous if the major Arab states settled their differences in time to present a united front to the incoming Administration. (Explaining the Syrian change of tack at Riyadh, the Damascus daily *Tishrīn* said on 24 October 1976 that since 1977 was likely to turn into a "decisive" year, "a common Arab will" was now needed.)

It was against this background that the Riyadh conference, often called "the restricted summit", covened—and succeeded. (An earlier meeting at Riyadh in June 1976, attended by the Syrian and Egyptian Prime Ministers at a time when the factors listed above did not yet operate, had ended in total failure, leaving the overall situation precisely as it had been.) The provisions worked out in Riyadh for a Lebanese ceasefire and eventual settlement are outside the scope of this essay (see survey of Lebanon). The preamble to the Riyadh declaration stated that the participants were "proceeding from the position of national and historic commitment to the need to strengthen the collective Arab role . . . from a desire to transcend the negative events and effects of the past [a reference mainly to the Egyptian-Syrian quarrel following the second Sinai Agreement], and from the need to go forward in a spirit of reconciliation, peace and reconstruction." A special resolution provided for the end of the propaganda war by laying down that "information campaigns and negative psychological mobilization by all parties should cease", and that information should be "channelled" so as to "raise the spirit of co-operation and fraternity among everyone."

Presidents Anwar Sādāt and Hāfiz al-Asad decided to reinstate their ambassadors in Damascus and Cairo (both had been demonstratively called home at the height of the quarrel in June 1976) and to "clear the atmosphere" between them.[1] To indicate why the atmosphere needed "clearing", it is instructive to recall two statements made only ten days before the Riyadh meeting. On the occasion of the anniversary of the October war, Sādāt had referred to Syria as being led by the "tangled rancorous ʻAlawite Baʻth Party"; at the same time a Baʻth Party statement had accused Egypt of "plotting" against Syria to "achieve the new objectives of imperialism and Zionism" and to rob the Arabs of their war gains.[2]

Answering questions put to him by an Egyptian journalist after the Riyadh conference, Asad said that "regardless of any difference that might occur" between himself and Sādāt, neither could "forget that they were partners in the [1973] October war." (This statement must be set against Asad's earlier accusations that during the war there had been US-Egyptian-Israeli collusion designed to produce a Syrian military debacle.)[3] Asad went on to say that he and Sādāt decided that Syrian-Egyptian relations will "remain stronger than any temporary and small differences, which soon disappear . . . The urgent tasks before us [i.e. mainly the co-ordination of Arab policies *vis-à-vis* the US] dictate that these relations remain strong and firm."[4]

Within a week, a full summit convened in Cairo. All Arab League nations took part, a fact worth noting, since some past summits had been boycotted by individual member-states. Algeria, Iraq, Libya, Morocco, Oman and Tunisia were not, however, represented by their heads of state, as the status of a summit conference, usually referred to by Arab media as a "meeting of the kings and presidents", would have required. The summit endorsed the Riyadh resolutions on 26 October.

It added a reference to the Arab Solidarity Pact of 15 September 1965, which had banned hostile propaganda and interference in internal affairs between Arab states, undertaking to abide by it "in full and forthwith." Moreover, it went beyond the Riyadh decision by establishing a special all-Arab fund to finance the "Arab security force" in Lebanon, which was made up almost exclusively of Syrian troops (see survey of Lebanon). The day after the conclusion of the summit, the Egyptian War Minister, Gen Muhammad 'Abd al-Ghanī Jamasī, was appointed supreme commander of the Egyptian-Syrian front—a post vacant since 1974. There was, however, hardly any public reference to this function during the remainder of the period reviewed here.

The manner in which the full summit acted almost solely as a "rubber stamp" for Riyadh once more underlined the drive and effectiveness of the Saudi initiative. The two countries clearly defeated by the broad Riyadh and Cairo censensus were Libya and Iraq. Only four months earlier they had made their bid to form a bloc with Syria, conditional on the latter *not* effecting a reconciliation with Egypt. These two let their displeasure be known in no uncertain terms. The Iraqi Foreign Minister, Sa'dūn Hammādi, who had represented Pres Ahmad Hasan al-Bakr at the summit, stated afterwards that his country had refused to ratify the Riyadh resolutions. The main reason for Iraq's stand, he explained, was that neither the restricted nor the full summit had provided for the withdrawal of Syrian forces from Lebanon, which Iraq deemed "essential"; Syria's intervention was "not impartial" but directed against one side in the Lebanese war. The Lebanese problem should have been remedied by truly "collective Arab actions."[5] Libya, for its part, had also attempted to press for the evacuation of Syrian troops from Lebanon during the summit debates. It later described the Cairo meeting as "a complete failure."

The restricted Riyadh summit and the full summit in Cairo set the basic pattern of inter-Arab relationships for a period of almost a year. This pattern can be characterized as follows:

1) Egypt, Syria and Saudi Arabia came once again to form the core triangle of inter-Arab action, as in 1973. Relations between them and their attitudes towards the rest of the Arab countries determined the *overall* texture of inter-Arab affairs.

2) All outward manifestations of the Syrian-Egyptian quarrel of 1975-6 ceased; but Syria continued to compete with Egypt, in muted tones and semi-concealed ways, for a more active and central inter-Arab role.

3) Syria gained factual recognition of its position as arbiter of Lebanese affairs, but had to contend with pro-PLO pressures exercised by Saudi Arabia, Egypt and Kuwait—the members, alongside Syria, in the ceasefire co-ordination committee set up under the Riyadh resolutions. Egypt no longer disputed Syria's role in Lebanon. Sādāt later said that after Riyadh, "Syrian action was no longer purely Syrian . . . We agreed to the entry of Syrian forces because they became part of the Arab deterrent force."[6] Asad, by contrast, stated in an interview with Radio Cairo on 17 December: "The truth of the matter is that the Arab deterrent force are basically Syrian forces."

4) Egypt gained (or perhaps more correctly regained) recognition as the principal Arab spokesman in addressing the West on the Arab-Israeli conflict—a position that remained virtually unchallenged until the visit to the Middle East of US Secretary of State, Cyrus Vance, in August 1977. It cannot be ruled out that Egypt achieved such status at Riyadh by a promise to Syria to jointly revive the military option against Israel should the "political process" fail to produce the results expected by the Arabs. (Egyptian, Syrian and Saudi references to the possibility of war in the event of renewed political stalemate were frequent in

1977, see below.)

5) Jordan, which before the Riyadh conference had seemed to be moving towards increasing dependence on Syria, gained more room for manoeuvre on the inter-Arab scene, particularly as between Egypt and Syria, and used it skilfully to reassert its position.

6) Saudi Arabia—making use of its political and Islamic leverage and its huge financial resources—fortified its position as a central factor in all-Arab affairs. It successfully promoted itself to the rank of a "confrontation state" (though not bordering on Israel, not directly affected by Security Council Resolution 242, not invited to the Geneva conference in 1973, and not a candidate for participation in its reconvention). Furthermore, having taken the lead in Arab affairs regarding the Persian Gulf in the early 1970s and in Southern Arabian affairs in the mid-seventies, it now extended its activities to the entire Red Sea area as well. The former editor-in-chief of Cairo's *Al-Ahrām*, Muḥammad Ḥasanayn Haykal, wrote: "The Arab world is now in what may be termed the Saudi epoch in modern Arab history."[7]

7) The "division of labour" between the three vertices of the "triangle"—as *Syria* perceived it—is indicated in the following comment from the Syrian daily *Al-Thawra* (20 May 1977): "Syria represents a major military power in the Middle East; Egypt a political power, and Saudi Arabia an oil power."

8) Through one or the other of its three member-states, further Arab countries came to be linked to the "triangle": Jordan has already been mentioned; the Lebanese government formed in 1976 came under Syrian tutelage as far as its inter-Arab contacts were concerned; and Sudan had formed close and formal ties with Egypt. Saudi influence was predominant in all the Arab littorals along the Persian Gulf, as well as in the Yemen Arab Republic (North Yemen); during 1977, Saudi Arabia was at work to bring the People's Democratic Republic of Yemen (South Yemen) into the fold of its Peninsular predominance (see also below). Morocco and Tunisia, perhaps mainly because of their local disputes with Algeria and Libya respectively, were also inclined to fall into line with the three central countries over matters of general policy.

9) Three Arab countries—Iraq, Libya and, in the North African context, Algeria—remained outside the constellation described above. During the period under review, each became—or continued to be—the initiator of private vendettas, all of which had an unsettling, if somewhat marginal, effect on the inter-Arab scene. Iraqi and Libyan activities also impinged on the domestic situation of their chief rivals: Syria, Egypt and Sudan (see surveys of these countries). All these disputes were characterized by a rising level of violence. (They will be referred to in greater detail presently.)

10) The PLO, saved from defeat and fragmentation by the Lebanese ceasefire, struggled on to preserve a minimal independent *military* presence and some freedom of action in Syrian-controlled Lebanon, but invested its main efforts in promoting its capacity for *political* manoeuvre by exploiting policy differences between the major Arab states.

A new topic came to preoccupy many of the inter-Arab meetings of 1976 and 1977: that of the Red Sea and its future as an "Arab lake." Growing attention to Red Sea affairs—comparatively speaking an innovation as a subject of inter-Arab dealings—was not a product of the changes brought about at Riyadh, but was primarily triggered by local events (the changes in Ethiopia; the independence of Djibouti) and the orientation of Somalia and Ethiopia towards the major powers. Considerations of the Red Sea's role in the Arab-Israeli conflict were not, however, absent from Arab deliberations on this subject (see essay on the Red Sea).

EGYPTIAN-SYRIAN RELATIONS

The first major step in Egyptian-Syrian relations reflecting the post-Riyadh atmosphere was Asad's visit to Cairo from 18-21 December 1976. In the interval, both sides had spoken of their relations in rather low-key terms. The Egyptian Premier, Mamdūḥ Sālim, said on 11 December, for instance, that "the resumption of Egyptian-Syrian relations at a level that satisfies the two peoples . . . portends good"; and Asad stated on 17 December: "We can say that we have at this stage been able to overcome the difficulties that stood in our way in the previous stage."[8]

The joint statement of 21 December 1976 used less restrained language. Again evoking the October war as the model, Syria and Egypt expressed their "sincere feeling of brotherhood" as well as "the unity of their objectives and comradeship in the struggle to achieve the goals of Arab nation . . . This was totally and magnificently expressed in the October War." The talks between "the two fraternal countries" took place "in an atmosphere of complete understanding." "Throughout history", the statement went on, Syria and Egypt had been "the shield of the Arab nation in confronting foreign schemes aimed at subjugating and dismembering it." The statement went on to outline a common strategy in the Arab-Israeli conflict, stressing Sādāt's and Asad's "determination that the year 1977 shall be a year of movement towards ending occupation and regaining the rights of the Palestinians."

The communiqué reaffirmed Sādāt's leading role in promoting the political approach as applicable to "the current stage of the struggle." At the same time, Syria attempted to ensure that Egypt would not overstep the boundaries of what Syria considered acceptable. Hence, for instance, a reference to maintaining a "firm position" on the 1974 Rabat summit resolutions regarding the PLO; and the appeal to both the US *and* the USSR to "clearly and expeditiously" submit their plans for peace in the Middle East. Hence, also the reference to the military option as implied in the phrase that after ten years of occupation "the Arab nation will use *all its resources* to end the status quo", later reinforced by mention in Syria's party daily *Al-Ba'th* (23 December 1976) of the significance of the Sādāt-Asad meeting for "the liberation struggle, whether by peaceful means or by war." (Similarly, Egyptian Foreign Minister Ismā'īl Fahmī: "We do not rule out . . . resorting to war if the [Israeli] enemy has not learned the lesson." Saudi Foreign Minister Sa'ūd al-Faysal: "If there is no settlement [by] the end of 1977 . . . Israel will succeed in imposing upon us a new military confrontation."[9]

In the field of bilateral relations, the two Presidents agreed to establish a Unified Political Command. The language of the joint declaration on this subject suggests that it was rather less than an operative decision: the command "shall lay down *as soon as possible* the necessary basis for . . . developing the relations of unity between the two countries . . . Joint committees . . . [shall] *study* and establish the bases on which relations of unity . . . can be developed in various fields."

The declaration was further watered down by the Egyptian Foreign Minister who stated that any other Arab state could join the command, since it was "meant to be the nucleus of a union that begins with Egypt and Syria." Only after studying the question of other states joining in would "the constitutional measures be completed."[10] In January 1977, in an address to the Egyptian People's Chamber, he further clarified the issue by saying that the command was "not the birth of a new unity but a declaration of intent." Eventually, "the question will be submitted to referendum so that any unionist step will be an offspring of the popular will."[11] Events soon bore out the notional character of the Command. In February 1977, Syria and Egypt appointed their representatives, but during the period reviewed (i.e. up to November 1977), it was not in fact convened. (Its notional existence should be compared to the more vigorous activities of similar Syrian-Jordanian bodies mentioned below.)

During the first eight months of 1977 there were numerous contacts between the two countries, both at bilateral and multilateral meetings, such as that between King Khālid, Asad and Sādāt in Riyadh on 19 May 1977. Major policy steps, particularly on questions relating to the Arab-Israeli conflict, were generally taken in consultation between the two countries. There was no mutual public criticism (Syrian newspapers, for instance, were on sale in Egypt again from April 1977 after a lengthy ban instituted during the earlier dispute). Yet a note of competition runs through the entire period. Syrian actions often marked off the difference of its policies from Egypt's, at least in detail. It was evident in Syria's continued consolidation of its influence in Lebanon and Jordan and over the PLO—a process which had been so salient a feature of the pre-Riyadh period. It showed in Syria's edging its way into the Egyptian-Sudanese joint command (see below) even though Sudan is not an area of primary interest to Syria. In May, the Syrian Prime Minister, 'Abd al-Raḥmān Khulayfāwī, said in an interview that Egyptian-Syrian relations "although good, are not as they should be." They should be "more comprehensive."[12]

While agreeing with Egypt in pressing for the speedy resumption of the Geneva conference, Syria differed over some aspects of tactics for its preparation. Already, at the time of the Asad-Sādāt meeting in December 1976, Syria had indicated a preference for the Arabs to be represented at Geneva by a single Arab delegation. At the time, and consistently for the rest of the period under review, Egypt opposed the idea. Syria may have hoped that, through its influence on the Jordanian, Palestinian and, possibly, the Lebanese members of the collective Arab delegation, it would have greater leverage on the conduct of the negotiations than by trying to co-ordinate independent missions. Primarily, however, it was Syria's desire to prevent any possibility of separate Egyptian-Israeli contacts which seems to have motivated Asad—a covert manifestation of the residual distrust towards Egypt, which had been so overt from the end of the October war until the Riyadh conference. It was resentment of this distrust, as well as unwillingness to have Egyptian diplomatic activity supervised or circumscribed, which led to Egyptian objections.

Another point was Syria's rejection of Egypt's exclusive orientation towards the US. Asad pointedly marked the difference by refusing to visit Washington as Sādāt did (4–7 April 1977); instead he chose to meet President Carter in Geneva on 9 May. Equally pointedly, Asad abstained from taking sides in the Soviet-Egyptian quarrel, keeping his own relations with the USSR much as they had been since the early 1970s. He "balanced" his meeting with Carter by a previous visit to Moscow (18–21 April 1977).

The latent differences between Egypt and Syria came out into the open again, more sharply than at any time since Riyadh, during the second Middle East visit of the US Secretary of State. On 2 August 1977, Sādāt—without prior consultation with Syria—suggested that Vance should prepare for the Geneva conference by setting up a "working group" of foreign ministers of all parties concerned, to meet in the US. Two days later, at the conclusion of Vance's visit to Damascus, Asad rejected the idea. Criticizing Sādāt for the first time in ten months, he told correspondents: "When brother Pres Sādāt proposed the formation of this [working] group . . . I do not know whether he has properly considered and assessed the negative aspects of this idea . . . Our brothers in Egypt . . . might see benefits in this working group of which we are not yet aware." Asad hastened to add: "The fact that we have not [previously] discussed this proposal does not mean that there are any differences between Syria and Egypt. Confidence between us is complete."[13] A few days later, Asad rejected the idea in firmer terms: "We shall not agree [to the working group] because we do not find within its terms anything constituting a gain for the Arab cause." He repeated Syria's longstanding preference for "a unified Arab delegation" to go to Geneva. Failing that, Syria, Egypt, Jordan and the PLO should be independently represented, "provided these delegations co-ordinate fully among themselves."[14]

Syria possibly suspected that Egypt might offer, or had already offered, the US greater concessions in moving towards the concept of "contractual peace" than Syria was willing to agree to—and might thus gain advantages for itself. Thus, if the Riyadh conference had revived the 1973 war partnership as the state of affairs to be aspired to between Egypt and Syria, the atmosphere a year later evoked the spectre of a new rift—such as had existed in 1975–6. As the party daily *Al-Ba'th* put it: "The coming phase will be dangerous [for Syria]; it will be a phase for exploding all the peripheral contradictions latent in the Arab area and to *re-explode those that have been patched up*"[15] (emphasis added). In short, if measured by the yardstick of converging or diverging policies towards Israel, Syrian-Egyptian relations seemed to have come full circle at that moment. This impression was reinforced the following month when Syria exploited an Arab League meeting (3–6 September) to propose a radical Arab line at the forthcoming UN General Assembly, including the expulsion of Israel from the UN and sanctions against it. Egypt opposed these proposals, terming them "insistence on the impossible", while Syria retorted by describing Egypt as "a prisoner of the US." Eventually, the immediate need to prepare for the Foreign Ministers' talks in the US later in September, caused the differences to be papered over. They were, however, not settled but merely postponed.

Another aspect of the overall relationship of the two countries was the continued consolidation of Syria's position of predominance in Lebanon, its special ties with Jordan, and its attempts to bend the PLO to its will. This policy line had been characteristic of Syria's inter-Arab stance in the period from the 1973 war to the 1976 Riyadh conference. At the time, it had a distinctly anti-Egyptian slant, aimed at downgrading Egypt's standing in all-Arab affairs and restricting its room of manoeuvre by virtually excluding it from any influence over the course of events in the areas adjacent to Syria. These included the geographical area of Palestine—which Asad had claimed to be "South Syria" in a speech in 1974—and which, in his eyes, the PLO represented politically. Sādāt had indeed interpreted this policy as being directed against Egypt and had—prior to the Riyadh conference—frequently referred to it as "suspect", a misguided Syrian ambition for all-Arab leadership.[16]

If Sādāt had hoped that the Riyadh agreement would put a stop to what he saw as the detrimental effects of this Syrian regional policy, he was disappointed. In Lebanon, the Syrians consolidated their military and political ascendancy to the point of leaving very little room for the intervention of third parties, as between Syria on the one hand and the various Lebanese groupings on the other. (For Syria's relations with these, see survey of Lebanon.) With respect to the PLO, Damascus did not have quite the same measure of success. Syria's attempts in establishing exclusive influence over the main PLO-establishment, particularly al-Fatḥ, were successful only in physical terms (gaining control of the areas around the main camps in Lebanon and, largely, over the supply routes feeding PLO bases). But attempts to block off PLO political leverage on other Arab states, or their political influence with the PLO, proved a failure. Throughout the period under review, the "rejectionist" groups in the PLO were able to appeal to Libya, Iraq and Algeria for support; and al-Fatḥ was able to capitalize on the subtle policy differences between Egypt, Syria and Saudi Arabia as far as the PLO was concerned. The following example relating to three concurrent trends which emerged within a single week in August 1977 may serve as an illustration. (The overall history of individual PLO relations with each of the major Arab states is outside the scope of this essay.)

1) During Vance's Middle East tour in August 1977, a report from Radio Beirut (2 August), most probably Syrian-inspired, spoke of an agreement having been reached by Syria and the PLO according to which "there shall be no links between the [Palestinian] state and Jordan before the Geneva conference . . .; moreover, any links with Jordan later on should be in the form of a confederation between Syria, Palestine and Jordan."

2) At the same time, Egypt (which had proposed the Palestinian-Jordanian link in the first place) ostentatiously convened the recently formed Higher Joint Egyptian-Palestinian Committee (including Yāsir 'Arafāt and Foreign Minister Fahmī), thus indicating that Egypt, rather than Syria, had taken the PLO under its wing. Egyptian spokesmen stressed that the Egyptian policies outlined to Vance had PLO support, and that Egypt was preparing the ground for US-PLO contacts.

3) At the same time, too, King Khālid and Crown Prince Fahd, also implying prior co-ordination with the PLO, made Saudi Arabia appear as the principal agent in taking action to bring the US and the PLO into official and openly-recognized contact.

Syria pursued its Jordanian alliance by successfully developing its policy of "integration", or *takāmul*, (the term used by both sides); yet, as will be presently described, "integration" reached a plateau in 1976 and levelled off in 1977. While Jordan clearly remained more closely tied to Syria than to any other Arab state throughout the period under review, this did not prevent King Ḥusayn from exploiting the "opening" towards Cairo with which the post-Riyadh constellation provided him. An account of Jordanian-Syrian and Jordanian-Egyptian relations will be given in the following sections. Their indirect, but considerable, impact on Syrian-Egyptian relations is important.

SYRIAN-JORDANIAN RELATIONS

Syrian-Jordanian relations had improved, at first almost imperceptibly, then by gradual steps, finally by leaps and bounds, ever since Asad came to power in Syria late in 1970. The new relationship found expression in the fact that in October 1973, Jordanian units joined the Syrian army in fighting the war on the Golan Heights. It entered into high gear in 1975, when the Joint Supreme Leadership Council (made up of King Ḥusayn and President Asad) and the Higher Jordanian-Syrian Joint Committee (headed by the two countries' prime ministers) were established. Slogans such as "one people—one country" or "one country—one people—one army" were used to create an atmosphere of an imminent union more far-reaching in an undefined way than the mere establishment of these two co-ordinating bodies. Meanwhile, a series of practical measures to "integrate" the activities of both states in economic spheres (joint planning and investments in industry and agriculture, mutual trade, joint customs policies), transportation (particularly border traffic), communications and education were put in hand. Over many such problems of a technical and day-to-day nature, the approach seems to have been eminently realistic and practical. Military co-ordination, though mentioned but rarely (for instance by Asad in an interview to Radio Cairo on 17 December 1976), was consistently promoted. (Traditionally, both Jordan and Syria have viewed the western reaches of their common border as an area particularly exposed to the danger of an Israeli military thrust.) It is noteworthy, however, that neither at the height of the use of unionist slogans nor later on, were measures taken which would have implied any erosion of the full and undisputed sovereignty of either country.

Political co-ordination had been close during 1975 and continued to remain so. Up to the Riyadh conference, it had paid off for Syria mainly in the wholehearted political and propaganda support which Jordan, alone in the Arab world, offered for Syria's intervention in Lebanon. During the talks leading to the 1976 Riyadh meeting, Syria had held out for Jordan's participation, but had eventually given way under pressure from the other participants who did not want a Ḥusayn-'Arafāt confrontation to add to the difficult tasks facing the conference. Asad took pains to "compensate" Ḥusayn by stopping over in Jordan for talks with the King, both on his way to Riyadh on 16 October 1976 and on his return three days later.

These frequent high-level contacts continued after the Riyadh conference. The Higher Jordanian-Syrian Joint Committee met in Damascus from 20-22 November 1976 and was mainly devoted to implementing decisions taken at its previous meeting in August 1976. Economic development, both agricultural and industrial, was a major item on the agenda. The concept of an industrial "division of labour" evolved, at least tentatively; the joint communiqué spoke of industrial projects to be "co-ordinated" so as to "avoid duplication." Joint committees were to study the scope of both Syria's and Jordan's investment programmes. The activites of the Jordanian-Syrian Industrial Company (established early in 1976) were to be intensified; the standardization of school curricula was to be expedited; measures to standardize codes of law and court procedure were to be taken in hand. The two Prime Ministers, Syria's 'Abd al-Raḥmān Khulayfāwī and Jordan's Mudar Badrān, "expressed their pride in the spirit of true brotherhood which had prevailed during the discussions."[17] Commenting on the meeting on 20 November, the Syrian Prime Minister spoke of the aspirations of the two countries to achieve "one day a form of union or federation."

A meeting of the Joint Supreme Leadership Council (the fourth since its establishment) took place in Amman from 6-8 December 1976 which from Asad's viewpoint, was to be part of his preparation for forthcoming talks in Cairo (postponed until 18 December because of Sādāt's illness, see above). Numerous press reports at the time speculated that the Council would conclude some federal project or similar form of institutionalized "unionist" scheme, the proclamation of which would enable Asad to meet Sādāt from a position of enhanced strength. The joint statement issued on 8 December did not, however, contain such a declaration. It said only that President Asad, King Ḥusayn and their most senior advisers had "made a general review of the co-ordination and integration steps . . . achieved so far . . . on the path of their cherished unity" and were determined "to continue the joint work." It asserted that "the steps . . . accomplished so far make it possible to proceed to a more advanced formula on the level of establishing joint institutions which will embody the common objective, and fulfil the aspirations of our one people in the two fraternal countries." (It was not specified what these institutions would be; but another joint committee was to continue "the general study" of future unionist steps and submit its conclusions "as soon as possible", so that the "relevant decisions will be taken and implemented in accordance with constitutional methods.")[18] With this meeting, the drive for Syrian-Jordanian "integration" seems to have passed its high point—at least temporarily. While Jordan had given unstinting support to Syria over the Lebanese issue as long as the Lebanese war lasted, Ḥusayn was not willing to grant Asad the same measure of support for the purpose of strengthening Syria's position *vis-à-vis* Egypt in the changed circumstances obtaining since the Riyadh conference. On the contrary, the results of that conference had made it possible for Jordan to think of some fence-mending in its relations with Egypt (a line Ḥusayn was promptly to pursue; see below), and the Jordanian leadership did not wish to enter this new stage with the onus of an overly specific commitment to Syria. The phrasing of the joint statement quoted above was thus a compromise, allowing Asad to proceed to Cairo with a reassertion of the special and far-reaching character of Syrian-Jordanian ties, yet not committing Jordan to any specific unionist step.

Beyond the divergent interests of the moment, however, there existed a more basic difference behind the somewhat equivocal phrasing of the above statement. Whatever Asad's precise ideas may have been concerning the long-term future of Syrian-Jordanian relations, Ḥusayn's concept certainly was that Jordan's sovereignty and ultimate freedom of action must not be compromised. The reference to "constitutional methods" was Ḥusayn's cautious, almost veiled, notice to Asad that whatever the future held for them, the King would not let his constitutional prerogatives in his own country be affected.

The issue of a possible federation continued to be mentioned, however. In January, for instance, Ḥusayn told the Jordanian cabinet that "steps towards a federation with sister Syria are continuing at a quick and steady pace." The "federation formula" should be capable of forming the "basis for a larger federation", as well as "harnessing the two countries' resources and potentials so that they may become a common asset for the two sides and for the Arab cause."[19] The following month, Premier Badrān referred to the union of Jordan and Syria: "We are studying every step scientifically, not emotionally."[20]

Although the process of "integration" levelled off towards the end of 1976, this did not mean there was a significant decrease in 1977. Even though slogans of the "one country—one people" type may have been used less frequently, and perhaps less fervently, in 1977 than in 1975 and 1976, the frequency of political consultation at the highest level and the routine work of practical co-ordination continued at the previous pace. In fact, co-operation during this period extended to matters of internal security: the visit to Amman on 13 December 1976 by President Asad's brother Rif'at (who held a leading position in internal affairs in Syria) was interpreted in the Arab press as being concerned with such an issue.

On 5 January 1977, Prime Minister Khulayfāwī met King Ḥusayn in Amman to review the unionist steps envisaged by Asad and Ḥusayn the month before. On 6 February, Husayn and Badrān visited Damascus. In Amman on 16 March, Ḥusayn again received Prime Minister Khulayfāwī, along with Foreign Minister (and Deputy Prime Minister) 'Abd al-Ḥalim Khaddām and Fawzī al-Kayyālī, the latter a representative of the National Progressive Front (the coalition of a number of minor Syrian parties which nominally shared power with the Ba'th). Arab and bilateral relations as well as the two countries' "unionist march" were discussed. Crown Prince Ḥasan headed a Jordanian delegation which visited Damascus from 12-14 April. On 8 May, a senior Jordanian court official met Asad in Geneva to report to him on Ḥusayn's talks with Carter in April, prior to Asad's meeting with the US President. On 18 May, Syrian Foreign Minister Khaddām reported to Jordanian leaders on Asad's meeting with Carter. On 22 June, Ḥusayn made another visit to Damascus.

From 30 June-3 July, the Higher Joint Committee met again in Amman. (The Committee's rules provide for meetings every three months. The interval from November 1976 to June 1977 was the first time that this rule was disregarded.) The Committee reviewed the work of the various sub-committees concerned with integration, and in its concluding statement "expressed its satisfaction with the great strides made by the joint . . . march towards its goal, which springs from the real will of the one people in the two fraternal countries to bypass artifical boundaries and to place their relations on a normal course." No concrete steps of political integration were mentioned, however, and the rest of the statement was devoted to questions of industrial and agricultural co-ordination, mutual trade, customs, transit, transportation, the joint use of electricity, tourism and education.[21] (See also, survey of Jordan.)

In summary, despite the successful promotion of co-ordination in all the *practical* fields listed above, basic views of the future *political* link between the two countries remained divergent. This was brought out strikingly early in August 1977 when Ḥusayn and Asad separately answered an identical question on a federation between Syria, Jordan and the West Bank. Ḥusayn termed the idea "farfetched"; Asad answered: "I am not against anything that reinforces Arab unity."[22]

JORDANIAN-EGYPTIAN RELATIONS

Up to the Riyadh conference in October 1976, Jordanian-Egyptian relations were overshadowed by the Syrian-Egyptian dispute. In accordance with the special Jordanian-Syrian ties which had evolved in 1975 and 1976, Jordan loyally supported Syria's inter-Arab policies, especially *vis-à-vis* Lebanon where Jordan had its own strong interest in seeing the PLO suppressed. Even at the time, though, it was noted that Jordan had not joined Syria in outright condemnation of Egypt's second Sinai Agreement.

When, after the Riyadh reconciliation, Jordanian overtures to Egypt could no longer be interpreted as disloyalty towards Syria, Egyptian-Jordanian relations improved quickly and to a considerable extent. Egypt's interest lay in prying Jordan loose, as far as possible, from its exclusive relationship with Syria—a development Sādāt believed would help him reassert Egypt's own inter-Arab position (in pursuit of the semi-concealed post-Riyadh competition with Syria, which has been referred to above). Sādāt's main leverage was in holding out hope for Jordan to regain—with Egypt's help—its standing in West Bank affairs: namely, that by co-operating with Egypt rather than Syria, Jordan might obtain a better, more direct, and less fettered position there. Reliance on Syria, on the other hand, would result in demands for a tripartite Syrian-Jordanian-Palestinian link which would amount to ultimate supervision from Damascus. One of the first signs of the changing relationship was the decision, in November 1976, to a mutual exchange of ambassadors. (Both embassies had been run by chargés d'affaires for approximately a year.)

In 1977, the highlights of improved bilateral ties were King Ḥusayn's two visits to Egypt, in January and July. During the first visit, from 13–15 January, the new constellation created at Riyadh was explicitly recognized: Ḥusayn "lauded the leading role played by Sādāt in moving the Arab issue", and "welcomed the closer links between fraternal Egypt and Syria" as likely to "solidify cohesion among the Arab confrontration states." Sādāt—accepting what he could no longer change—"welcomed the developing unionist steps between Syria and Jordan."

The joint statement again evoked "the momentum which resulted from the glorious October war" of 1973 (as had the statements issued after the Riyadh and Cairo meetings and the Sādāt-Asad talks). Sādāt and Ḥusayn expressed faith in a "unified Arab strategy" and in "co-ordination of the front-line forces." The main pointer to the give and take which must have proceeded behind closed doors was the phrase referring to the rights of the Palestinians to an "independent political entity." The Egyptians would at this time usually have referred to a "Palestinian state" rather than an entity; Ḥusayn might have preferred the term "political entity" without mention of its being "independent." The term "Palestinian state" appeared lower down in the statement in the context of Jordan's "disposition . . . to establish the *closest* relations with the Palestinian state" to be decided upon "by the two peoples [the Jordanian and the Palestinian] through their free choice" (i.e. not necessarily through the PLO). The PLO was mentioned in the statement only in relation to the Geneva conference.[23] The language chosen indicates both the readiness to compromise for the sake of improved relations, and the constraints circumscribing such a compromise for both sides.

On his return home, Ḥusayn explained that Jordanian-Syrian co-operation and Egyptian-Jordanian co-operation had become "complementary and served a common objective."[24] In another interview, he referred to his meeting with Sādāt as the "crowning of co-ordinated Arab efforts . . . to achieve Arab solidarity . . . to attain an assured victory peacefully or to resort to various possibilities if peace efforts fail."[25]

In the interval between Ḥusayn's January and July visits, with the US Administration launching a new initiative in the Middle East, Sādāt repeatedly referred to the ties which he thought should link the future Palestinian entity to Jordan. There remained some lack of clarity whether, on the question of timing, he sided with the PLO (who demanded a Palestinian state *first*, which would decide on the nature of its links with Jordan only *after* independence), or with Ḥusayn (who envisaged the reverse sequence, e.g. by means of reviving, in June 1977, the 1972 plan for a federation of the East and West Banks (for details, see survey of Jordan).

Ḥusayn's second meeting with Sādāt took place in Alexandria on 9 and 10 July. For the sake of "even-handedness", it had been preceded by a visit to Damascus at the end of June (see above), and by a trip to Riyadh earlier in July (see below). Sādāt again suggested "a clear link" between "the Palestinians and the Jordanians", to be established in advance of a Geneva conference. Ḥusayn, interpreting this as an attempt to pressure him into a reconciliation with the PLO, objected to the proposal. He argued that such ties with the Palestinians, while "inevitable" in themselves, should only be formulated after Israel's withdrawal and after "the Palestinian people practice . . . their right of self-determination" (again implying that this should be done independently of the PLO). No joint statement was issued on this occasion, reflecting the absence of substantive agreement on this point.[26] The Egyptian Foreign Minister, Ismā'īl Fahmī, stated that Ḥusayn and Sādāt had agreed to increase their contacts with the aim of a "further unification of stands."[27] Yet, at the time of Secretary Vance's visit the following month, and with the emergence of the Egyptian-Syrian differences over the proposal for a Foreign Ministers' "working group", Jordan sided with Syria rather than Egypt. With all the increased "elbow room" Jordan had been able to acquire during the last quarter of 1976 and the first half of 1977, its primary obligation, at a juncture of major import, remained to Syria. This remained true until November 1977.

SAUDI RELATIONS WITH JORDAN, SYRIA AND EGYPT

Saudi Arabia kept up a constant stream of high-level contacts with the three confrontation states. (For Saudi activities in other areas of the Arab world, see below.) Among visits to Saudi Arabia were those of Jordanian Prime Minister Mudar Badrān (on 15 December 1976 and again on 14 April 1977); King Ḥusayn (18 December 1976; and again on 6–7 July 1977); Ḥusayn's Chief of the Royal Cabinet 'Abd al-Ḥamīd Sharaf (on 29–30 March, 16 May and 30 July 1977); Syrian Foreign Minister 'Abd al-Ḥalīm Khaddām (13 February, 16 and 30 April and 14 May 1977; on 20 April, Khaddām visited King Khālid in London); Syrian Deputy Defence Minister Nājī Jamīl (27 July 1977); Egyptian Vice-President Ḥusnī Mubārak 17 November 1976); and Egyptian Deputy Premier for Financial and Economic Affairs 'Abd al-Mun'im al-Qaysūnī (24 March 1977).

Saudi visits to Arab capitals included Crown Prince Fahd's trip to Cairo (22 November 1976); Foreign Minister Sa'ud al-Faysal's visits to Cairo (4–5 February

1977, in connection with Saudi financial aid to Egypt); Damascus (1 March 1977); and his tour of Egypt, Jordan and Syria (beginning 7 June 1977) to report to their leaders on Amir Fahd's visit to Europe and the US in May. King Khālid's special adviser, Kamāl Adham, visited Cairo on 29 March, 16 June and 5 August; Damascus on 8 January and 1 March; and Amman on 8 January and 13 August 1977. The August visits were connected with the current Middle East tour of the US Secretary of State.

Furthermore, on two major occasions, Saudi Arabia hosted multilateral Arab meetings. The first, in Riyadh on 9–10 January 1977, was attended by the Foreign Ministers of Egypt, Syria, Jordan, Saudi Arabia, Kuwait, Qatar, the UAE and by a PLO representative. It dealt with the issue of financial assistance by the "supporting" states to the "front-line" states. This meeting, and possibly the follow-up one held less than a week later in Cairo, seem to have resulted in a re-affirmation on the part of the supporting states that the monetary assistance decided upon at the 1974 Rabat summit conference was a continuing obligation and not limited to a single year, as the recipients had feared. As is often the case with discussions of Arab monetary aid, no details or figures were released by the participants.

In the following months, there was occasional guarded criticism of Saudi Arabia on the part of Egypt, Syria and Jordan, hinting at insufficient financial support reaching them from Riyadh, as well as from other oil-producing Arab states. In March, a "responsible Saudi source expressed regret at [such] misrepresentations" which were likely to "benefit only the enemy."[28]

The second Riyadh meeting, on 19 May 1977, was attended by Presidents Asad and Sādāt and King Khālid. Originally initiated to co-ordinate Arab policies in advance of Amir Fahd's visit to Washington later the same month (a visit considered crucial by the leaders of the confrontation states), it was in fact overshadowed by the results of the Israeli election held on 17 May. It was on this occasion that a Radio Riyadh comment (in contrast to the station's traditionally reticent and non-committal line) spoke of Syria, Egypt and Saudi Arabia as the three "most powerful states in the region", adding that Saudi Arabia "enjoys a distinguished political and economic position." Fahd's US visit, the commentator went on, would "decide much of the future of the whole Arab region."[29] According to Egyptian sources, the views expressed at the meeting by the three leaders on US-Arab relations, on ties with USSR and on the Israeli elections, were "identical", and there was "complete understanding."[30]

In view of the general reticence of the three or four really significant spokesmen of the Saudi regime, any attempt to assess basic Saudi trends and objectives on the inter-Arab scene requires an element of speculation. Extreme caution in making public statements has been a deliberate Saudi policy. Its Defence Minister, Amir Sultān Ibn 'Abd al-'Azīz, told an interviewer: "Saudi abstention from entering into vocal public exchanges is one of the main reasons for [our] success at the Riyadh conference."[31] What is clear—from Saudi actions rather than declarations—is that King Khālid and Amir Fahd were, during the period under review, determined to use all of Saudi Arabia's assets—its guardianship of Mecca and Medina and of Islamic traditions; its financial power; its ability to wield the "oil weapon" or refrain from doing so; its influence in the US; its fast-increasing role as an arms arsenal for other Arab countries and as financier of their own arms procurement programmes—in order to propel itself into a position of ultimate arbiter of all-Arab political affairs. Not taking sides in Arab disputes was also an explicit Saudi policy. As Amir Fahd described it: "Saudi Arabia does not believe in the system of [Arab] axes or blocs. It has never taken part in any political axis."[32]

More speculative is the assessment of the place and role of the confrontation states in the Saudi scheme of things. It would probably be correct to say that Riyadh would wish Egypt and Syria to be aligned but not closely allied (so that both would look to Saudi Arabia to keep the alignment intact despite an undercurrent of rivalry); that Egypt should remain preoccupied with (but not endangered by) domestic difficulties and the conflict with Israel, so as to preclude any revival of a forward, activist pan-Arab policy on its part ('Abd al-Nāsir's designs in the Arabian Peninsula are unlikely to be quite forgotten in Riyadh); that Syria should remain engaged in building its own sphere of influence, but should not quite succeed; and that Jordan should have a standing in the West Bank and Gaza, balanced by the presence of that part of the PLO which the Saudis trust, i.e. Al-Fatḥ, to the exclusion of the leftist "rejectionist" groups.

The period from the 1976 Riyadh conference until the autumn of 1977 was one in which these objectives were in the process of being effectively promoted, though their final consummation remained to be achieved.

IRAQI-SYRIAN RELATIONS

Outside the "core triangle", the first set of developments to be reviewed is that of Iraqi-Syrian relations. As already mentioned, Iraq's principal explicit criticism of the October 1976 Cairo summit was that it had sanctioned Syria's military presence in Lebanon. The stress Iraq placed on this particular aspect of the Riyadh and Cairo decisions reflected the consistently anti-Syrian line which Iraq had taken during the Lebanese civil war. With the exception of a short period in the summer of 1976 (when Iraq had hoped to exploit Asad's military and political difficulties in Lebanon to draw him into a bloc with Libya, Algeria, the PLO and itself), Iraq had tried to foil Syria's Lebanese policy at every turn. It had used all forms of propaganda warfare to make Syria's motives in Lebanon appear suspect, and had given political and material support to every Lebanese and PLO group resisting Syria's intervention (including, in 1976, the dispatch of a small contingent of Iraqi army troops to Lebanon).

Iraq's stand on the Lebanese issue was, however, only one of the many facets of its fundamental hostility to Syria. Geo-political and historical arguments of a somewhat speculative character have often been adduced to explain the frequent periods of tension between Baghdad and Damascus. In the present-day context, it would be correct to say that the current Syrian-Iraqi animosity dates back to 1968 when Pres Aḥmad Ḥasan al-Bakr's wing of the Ba'th party came to power in Baghdad. Bakr had been expelled from the Syrian-dominated Ba'th Party in 1966 for being a "rightist." With his ascent to power there came into being two ruling Ba'th parties—in Syria and in Iraq—each claiming to be the "real", "original" and "genuine" one, and each disputing the legitimacy of the other and, by implication, the legitimacy of its authority in the other's country.

Asad's rise to power in Syria in November 1970 further aggravated Iraqi-Syrian relations. Asad's inter-Arab policies from 1971–3—guided by pragmatism and expediency rather than by Ba'thi ideology and doctrine—brought about a Syrian-Egyptian *rapprochement*, as well as improved Syrian relations with Jordan and Saudi Arabia. They thus accentuated the relative isolation on the Arab scene in which Iraq had found itself during most of the early and middle 1970s.

The conclusion of the 1973 war brought further deterioration. Iraqi troops had taken part in the fighting on the Syrian front; but when hostilities ended, Iraq scathingly criticized Syria for accepting the ceasefire and, later, for concluding the Golan Heights disengagement agreement (May 1974), and for participating in the series of political contacts with the US initiated in the aftermath of the war. Iraqi references to Syria's "capitulationist" and "defeatist" attitude and its "collaboration with Imperialism" remained part of the propaganda exchanges in 1976 and 1977; so did Syria's descriptions of the Iraqi regime as "fascist", "oppressive" and "slogan-bound."

Shortly before the Syrian-Iraqi controversies began focusing on Lebanon, tension reached a particular peak in the spring of 1975. Its immediate cause was the question of the distribution of the Euphrates River waters, but its acrimony stemmed from the broader underlying issues referred to above. Iraq asserted that Syria had operated the Tabaqa dam across the upper Euphrates in northern Syria (built between 1968 and 1973 with Soviet aid) so as to deprive Iraq of its share of river water and to prevent the implementation of its agricultural development schemes. Syria denied the Iraqi charges. As the recriminations intensified, Iraq concentrated troops in the border area and Syria followed suit. During the summer of 1975, both sides gradually reduced their concentrations, the crisis atmosphere abated and eventually both armies returned to their usual areas of deployment. The Euphrates waters issue, however, remained unresolved.

At about the same time, in mid-1975, Iraq made one of its periodic attempts to draw Syria into a radical "rejectionist" alliance based on an Iraqi commitment to place troops on the Golan Heights in return for Syria's rejection of Security Council Resolution 242, its refusal to participate in the Geneva conference and, generally, a return to what the Iraqis termed "the path of struggle." A similar attempt had been made in 1972; another was to follow in 1976. But Syria ignored the Iraqi initiative and soon afterwards, in the autumn of 1975, Iraq became the first Arab country to come out in vocal criticism of Syria's role in the Lebanese war.

In April 1976, Iraq added a form of economic warfare to her other anti-Syrian activities: it stopped the transit of oil through the pipeline running across Syria to the Mediterranean, pumping it instead through a new pipeline to the Persian Gulf. Syria lost transit dues estimated at close to $500m annually (a loss all the more keenly felt as Syria's intervention in the Lebanese war was becoming increasingly expensive).

Syria's massive entry into Lebanon in the first week of June 1976 was followed by a renewal of Iraqi troop concentrations on the Syrian borders. Both Pres Bakr and spokesmen for his regime said the troops were "ready to enter Syria" to prepare for "the liberation of Palestine" (as part of the revival, in May and June, of the "rejectionist" bloc scheme; see above). In fact, they were intended to deter Syria from continuing the occupation of Lebanon, or at least to slow it down. When this proved patently unsuccessful, a subtler struggle developed between the two countries with both parading military and civilian defectors, who described the "treasonable activities" of the rival regime. The Syrian defectors spoke of Asad "crushing" the PLO and suppressing the "Lebanese National Movement": the Iraqi defectors of their country's sabotaging Syrian efforts to restore peace in Lebanon. Syria accused the Iraqis of involvement in a series of attacks by a group called the "Black June Organization", which claimed that it was taking revenge against Syria for acts it had committed against Palestinians in Lebanon. "Black June" operations included an attack against the Semiramis Hotel in Damascus (26 September) and against the Syrian embassies in Rome and Islamabad (11 October 1976).

In the new constellation created in October by the Riyadh conference, Egypt, which until then had sided with Iraq in opposing Syria's intervention in Lebanon (though not over any other issue of Arab politics), now resigned itself to the new realities; Libya became more and more engrossed in the quarrels with its neighbours (see below); and Algeria withdrew increasingly into North African affairs, particularly the Western Sahara imbroglio. Iraq thus remained Syria's sole active opponent.

On 26 October (the concluding day of the Cairo summit conference), a transmitter calling itself "The Voice of Arab Syria" began broadcasting a daily programme purporting to present the viewpoint of Syrian leftists opposed to Asad. It called on the Syrian people to overthrow Asad's regime, and on the Lebanese to rise against the "Syrian invaders." Although the station did not disclose its location, it was almost certainly situated in Iraq. It was Radio Baghdad which announced the inception of the transmitter's broadcasts; the station's first comment praised Iraq's stand at the summit conference and denounced that of Syria, and subsequent reports echoed Iraqi views and attitudes. The Iraqi News Agency frequently cited "The Voice of Arab Syria" and quotations from its transmissions became one of Iraq's chief instruments in continuing anti-Syrian propaganda regarding Lebanon. In an effort to curtail other Iraqi propaganda outlets, Syrian troops occupied the offices of pro-Iraqi newspapers in Beirut in December 1976. In the same month, Lebanese sympathizers of the Iraqi Ba'th were arrested by the Syrians. On the other hand, the Iraqi military measures were now called off. After the ceasefire in Lebanon came into force, it became pointless to try and pin down Syrian troops opposite the Iraqi border. During November 1976, Iraqi forces were withdrawn from the border area and Syria followed suit. By the end of the year, most of the Iraqi regulars who had joined the PLO and their Lebanese allies in Lebanon were repatriated as well.

As the situation in Lebanon quietened down late in 1976 and in 1977, Iraq's anti-Syrian propaganda began to stress other themes. Allegations against Syria of following a "capitulationist policy" in the Arab-Israeli conflict and of "betraying the Palestinians" now became central motifs. The UNDOF mandate renewals in November 1976 and May 1977, Asad's meeting with Carter in May 1977, and Secretary of State Vance's visits to Damascus in February and August 1977 were made to serve as special occasions for such charges. The "renegade" character of the Syrian "agent regime" was contrasted with Iraq's "principled", "nationalist" and "progressive" stand. Iraqi media accused Syria of arresting and killing PLO leaders as well as rank and file members, both in Lebanon and in Syria. They pointed to Syria's relations with Jordan as proof of Asad's accommodation with "Arab reactionary forces." Referring to Syrian domestic policies, Iraqi media and spokesmen charged the regime with "arbitrary detention of innocent civilians and members of the armed forces", and with the assassination of many of the detainees.

Syrian propaganda countered by blaming Iraq for "deviating from Arab solidarity", a role which was "in harmony with the Zionist imperialist aims in the Arab area."[33] The principal line of Syrian propaganda, however, dealt with Iraqi internal policies and particularly with the personal role of Saddām Ḥusayn, President Bakr's right-hand man. Ḥusayn (originally Saddam Ḥusayn al-Tikrītī) was referred to by the Syrian media as "the head of the ruling clique in Baghdad", or of "the Tikrītī tribal (or family) regime", a reference to the fact that many prominent figures of the Iraqi Ba'th regime come from the town of Tikrīt. Described as the leader of a "regime of murderers", Ḥusayn was declared responsible for the persecution and, in many cases, the liquidation of Iraqi citizens without trial. Adding an appeal for action to these accusations, a Syrian Ba'th National Command member called on the people of Iraq "to escalate the struggle against fascism" and to rally around the Iraqi "nationalist movement" which was "waging the struggle for a free Iraq."[34] A radio commentary stated that "the killers in Baghdad will be dealt with by the justice of [the Arab] people in Iraq as it has dealt with Nūrī al-Sa'īd, 'Abd al-Karīm Qāsim [assassinated in the Iraqi coups of

1958 and 1963 respectively] and other traitors."[35]

The stoppage of oil transit from Iraq through Syria (which seemed to acquire a permanent character in January 1977, when a second Iraqi pipeline to the Mediterranean was inaugurated which passed entirely through *Turkish* territory) was also exploited by the Syrian media for anti-Iraqi propaganda. By depriving Syria of the transit dues, they argued, Iraq was diminishing Syria's capacity to "carry on the struggle" and was "brandishing against an Arab country" the oil weapon that should be wielded against Israel.[36] In an attempt to apply economic counter-measures, Syria stopped the transit of goods from Syrian ports to Iraq in December 1976.

Propaganda warfare and economic pressures apart, almost every sign of unrest, disaffection or political discontent in either country was attributed by it to subversive activities on the part of the other. Syria blamed Iraqi agents for the attempt on the life of Foreign Minister 'Abd al-Ḥalīm Khaddām (1 December 1976); for the assassination of Muḥammad al-Fādil, President of Damascus University and a prominent Ba'th party functionary (22 February 1977); and for a number of explosions at public buildings in Damascus and near the homes of several leading figures in the regime (July 1977). (For this and other aspects of the internal security situation in Syria, see survey of Syria.) The Syrian government newspaper claimed that Saddām Husayn was heading a special bureau in Baghdad planning and supervising acts of assassination and sabotage in Syria.[37]

Similarly, Iraq accused Syria of responsibility for an explosion which occurred at Baghdad airport on 14 December 1976. More significantly, perhaps, the Iraqi spokesman also blamed Syrian agitators for widespread riots among the Shī'ī population in southern Iraq in February 1977 (see survey of Iraq). The riots had been triggered, so the Iraqi government announced, by the explosion of a bomb placed at the Al-Ḥusayn mosque in Karbalā—the city holy to Shī'īs—by a Syrian agent. Renewed unrest in Iraqi Kurdistan (see survey of Iraq) was also at times blamed by Iraq on Syrian encouragement of Kurdish insurgents.

Both Syria and Iraq denied charges of being engaged in subversive activities on their neighbour's territory. Instead, they pointed to violations of internal security as proof of the existence of widespread *domestic* opposition against the regime existing there. At the time of the changes in the Iraqi RCC (see survey of Iraq), Damascus Radio commented that "the power struggle in Iraq had entered a serious phase" and predicted that Saddām Ḥusayn's next move would be made against Bakr.[38]

By and large, during the period reviewed, it was Iraq which took the initiative, and Syria which was on the defensive in the quarrel (though elsewhere the opposite was usually true). Although each had to pay a price for the maintenance of the dispute, in terms of inter-Arab and domestic political difficulties and economic losses, the price of reconciliation seemed higher in comparison. As President Bakr stated in a speech on the anniversary of his 1968 takeover: "We will not hold out our hand to those [in Syria] who have deviated from . . . the pan-Arab struggle . . ., cheaply conspired against their brothers and massacred our Palestinian and Lebanese brothers just as the Zionists have done."[39]

It is noteworthy that the outside Arab world seemed to share the assessment that, as long as Asad and Bakr were in power, Syrian-Iraqi hostility would persist. While every other inter-Arab dispute elicited frequent and persistent Arab mediation attempts, the complete absence of any Arab effort, in 1976 and 1977, to bring about a Syrian-Iraqi conciliation speaks for itself.

LIBYAN RELATIONS WITH EGYPT AND SUDAN

Like Iraq, Libya found its inter-Arab standing damaged by the Riyadh conference.

Having been cut off from the mainstream of Arab events as long ago as 1973, its isolation now became greater and more manifest. In the immediate pre-Riyadh period, i.e. during the Syrian-Egyptian quarrel of 1975 and 1976, Libya had regarded Syria as at least a potential ally against Egypt and had believed the dispute useful to Libya in its own attempts to challenge Sādāt's leadership. Even in the summer of 1976, when the attempt to draw Syria into a bloc with Iraq, Algeria, the PLO and Libya itself, had failed, Libya still refrained from publicly criticizing Syria. After the Syrian-Egyptian reconciliation of October 1976, however, Libya was left as Egypt's only active Arab adversary in much the same way as Iraq had remained alone in active opposition to Syria.

Furthermore, the Riyadh conference brought into sharper focus the fact that while Syrian-Egyptian differences found expression mainly in political pressures and propaganda warfare, the Libya-Egyptian quarrel assumed the form of subversive activities carried out by each government inside the territory of its neighbour. This was facilitated by the fact of geographical proximity which made across-the-border infiltration possible. But it also reflected different objectives: Syria's anti-Egyptian campaign had been directed against Sādāt's policies and was intended to restrict Egypt's influence in inter-Arab affairs; Libya's actions were meant to undermine Sādāt's power at home and, ultimately, to cause his overthrow (Sādāt retaliated in kind).

Mu'ammar al-Qadhdhāfī's personal vindictive attitude towards Sādāt went back to the latter's rise to power after 'Abd al-Nāsir's death in 1970. An ardent Nāsir disciple, Qadhdhāfī now came to regard himself as Nāsir's potential heir, particularly with regard to the pan-Arab aspect of Nasserist ideology. Concomitantly, he came to dispute Sādāt's claim to be 'Abd al-Nāsir's true successor. Nonetheless, until 1973, Qadhdhāfī hoped to gain the Arab role he believed to be his due by co-operating with Sādāt, expecting that eventually he would be able to make Egypt his springboard to all-Arab leadership. In 1971, Qadhdhāfī was instrumental in establishing the Federation of Arab Republics (of Egypt, Libya and Syria). When the Federation remained void of political content, he began in 1972 to press for a complete merger of Egypt and Libya into a single state. Libyan pressure continued until the eve of the 1973 October war, when Sādāt finally turned down the merger idea.

In preparing for and launching the 1973 war, Egypt as well as Syria completely ignored Libya. Qadhdhāfī for his part criticized the decision to go to war, derided its objectives and described its outcome as totally negative for the Arab cause. From then on, relations between Egypt and Libya deteriorated fast. In 1975, they were further aggravated by a Libyan about-face which was to have strong repercussions in the period under review: Libya, till then strongly anti-Soviet, signed a major arms deal with the USSR—a step which Sādāt interpreted as anti-Egyptian on the part of Libya, as well as on the part of the USSR.

Increasingly, in 1975 and 1976, both Egypt and Libya turned to measures designed to weaken their rival's domestic situation. Libya began to support and encourage discontented groups of a traditional Islamic character within Egypt. For her part, Egypt granted asylum to Libyan political exiles. Most prominent among them was Major 'Umar al-Muḥayshī, a former Libyan RCC member, who had fled the country after an abortive coup in the summer of 1975. Muhayshī was offered Egyptian broadcasting facilities to conduct anti-Qadhdhāfī propaganda and frequently appealed to Libyans to overthrow their regime. According to Libyan sources, Egypt was also exploiting members of the Egyptian work force in Libya for purposes of subversion. (Egyptian labourers, tradesmen and professionals had been brought in by Qadhdhāfī in substantial numbers between 1970 and 1973. By 1975, they had turned into a political liability, but economic realities did not permit him to dispense with them.)

Another factor which in the mid-1970s began to influence Egyptian-Libyan and, eventually, Libyan-Sudanese relations was the steady improvement in Egyptian-Sudanese ties during the period. In part at least, Egypt sought closer ties with Sudan in order to strengthen its position *vis-à-vis* Libya and, conversely, Qadhdhāfī viewed this *rapprochement* as a hostile act on the part of both Sudan and Egypt. In February 1974, Sādāt and the Sudanese President, Ja'far Numayrī, met and agreed on a programme of political co-ordination and economic co-operation. A Joint Higher Ministerial Committee was formed to discuss specific joint projects. It was to meet twice a year, but actually convened only four times in the first three and a half years of its existence. Nevertheless, the alignment soon produced palpable results: Sudan fully supported Egypt's policies in the conflict with Israel and, like Egypt, gradually turned towards the US; joint projects in the fields of agriculture, (irrigation, land reclamation and cultivation), industry, communications and transport, health, education and information were discussed, and some were launched.

Libya, which in July 1971 had given Numayrī valuable assistance in putting down a leftist coup attempt, now began to exploit the precarious domestic situation of the Sudanese regime by offering refuge to Sudanese political expatriates and potential opposition activists. In 1974 and again in 1975, both Numayrī and Sādāt attributed coup attempts in Sudan to Libyan planning and instigation. Another more dangerous attempt occurred in 1976 and forms the immediate background to events during the period under review. In July 1977, Numayrī barely escaped an attempt on his life during a bloody but eventually abortive coup. Egypt sent immediate aid to Khartoum and joined Sudan in blaming Libya for training and equipping the rebels and helping them infiltrate across the border into Sudan. Libya rejected the accusations, claiming that indigenous groups within Sudan had carried out the insurrection alone. (For the nature of opposition to Numayrī, see survey of Sudan.)

On 15 July 1976, in the wake of the coup attempt, Egypt and Sudan signed a joint defence agreement for which, a few days later, they received implicit Saudi blessing. The agreement stipulated that armed aggression against either state or its armed forces would be considered an aggression against both. The two states would "unify" military planning and operations in case of danger. They would set up a Joint Defence Council to meet every six months or when necessitated by circumstances, and a joint staff, to meet at least every three months. The signature was followed by a meeting of the Defence Council (in Cairo, from 7–9 September) and of the two chiefs of staff (in Khartoum, from 6–8 November 1976) when the implementation of the agreement was discussed. (The Defence Council did not meet again during the period reviewed; the chiefs of staff held a second meeting, in Cairo, from 23–26 April 1977.) Immediately after the signing of the defence agreement, Egyptian troops estimated at 10,000 men and including infantry, armour, artillery, and air defence units were concentrated close to the Libyan border. Further reinforcements reached the border area in August and September 1976.

On 8 August, a bomb exploded at a centrally-located government building in Cairo; on 14 August 1976, an explosive charge went off on a train about to leave Alexandria for Cairo. Casualties resulted in both cases. The Egyptian authorities arrested a number of Libyan nationals for both acts, as well as charging Egyptians with having acted under Libyan orders. The Libyans at the same time arrested a number of Egyptians for espionage, subversion and incitement against the regime and for planning acts of sabotage. Egyptian leaders now justified the troop concentrations by pointing out that Libya was setting up training bases for saboteurs close to the border, as well as command posts for directing their forays into Egypt.

Hostile propaganda was stepped up by both sides: a Radio Cairo comment said that "the time has come to put an end to [Qadhdhāfī's] rule"; the Libyan news agency stated that, since Sādāt had "degenerated to the lowest bottom of treason" there was "no justification for his being at the head of the great Egyptian Arab people."[40] Qadhdhāfī accused Egypt of endangering the Sinai front by moving troops into the Western Desert.[41] Sādāt, who had until then referred to Qadhdhāfī as "sick", now called him a "madman." Qadhdhāfī himself did not attack Sādāt personally, but the Libyan media spoke of him as a hashish addict, and named him "the khedive of Egypt", thus evoking associations of feudalism, corruption and subservience to imperialistic overlords.

Qadhdhāfī, while also reinforcing the units holding the Libyan side of the border, apparently hoped at that time to prevent an armed clash. In his Revolution Day speech on 1 September 1976, he announced that relations with Egypt would not be severed, that Libya "will not fight the Egyptian army", and that only those Egyptian workers in Libya who had been enlisted by the Egyptian intelligence service would "pay the price"; the others would continue to live honourably "among their Libyan brothers."[42] Some 30 Egyptians detained in Libya on suspicion of agitation or acts of sabotage were released to mark Revolution Day. Sādāt, however, was not appeased. In interviews and speeches in August and September, he said of Qadhdhāfī: "This time he will not get out from my hands."[43]

In the immediate wake of the Riyadh conference in October, tension abated somewhat. Part of the Egyptian forces were transferred back from the Libyan border to the Suez Canal. Propaganda attacks became less frequent and at the beginning of December 1976, each country allowed the entrance of its neighbour's newspapers, after a ban of two years. The lull was to prove short-lived.

Egypt was now mainly concerned with fostering its new relations with Syria and Jordan, but continued to promote co-ordination with Sudan as well. From 21-23 November 1976 and again from 26-28 May 1977, the Egyptian-Sudanese Joint Higher Ministerial Committee met to review the implementation of previous decisions and to recommend new joint projects. Numayrī visited Cairo from 19-21 May for talks with Sādāt. During this period, Egyptian and Sudanese leaders frequently stressed that the July 1976 defence agreement had added a new dimension to their mutual ties. Egyptian Foreign Minister Fahmī called it a "shining example of wise unionist action", adding that it extended the "strategic depth" of both countries and was "a shield to Sudan against its enemies."[44]

From the beginning of 1977 onwards, Ethiopia came to be numbered as another enemy of Sudan, alongside Libya. Sudan claimed that, with Libyan assistance, camps serving Numayrī's opponents were being set up in Ethiopia close to the Sudanese border. Sudanese opposition elements were now allowed to cross into Sudan from there, in addition to others infiltrating across the Libyan-Sudanese frontier. In January 1977, Egypt declared its support for Sudan against Ethiopia as well as against Libya. (For the effect of developments in Ethiopia on Arab attitudes in the Red Sea area in general, and towards Eritrea in particular, see below.)

Libya's resentment over Egyptian ties with Sudan was further aroused in January 1977 when Egypt and Syria announced that their Unified Political Command (see above) would be extended to embrace Sudan as well. Sādāt, Asad and Numayrī indeed met in Khartoum on 27-28 February 1977 and issued a joint declaration making Sudan a party to the command.[45] The decision underlined the existing political alignments and added to Numayrī's prestige, particularly at home. In practice, however, the enlarged Unified Political Command had not been formed by November 1977. Syria did not take sides in the subsequent stages of the Egyptian-

Libyan and Sudanese-Libyan disputes, and Egypt and Sudan continued to handle their problems bilaterally. Nonetheless, Qadhdhāfī continued to be strongly critical of Sudanese-Egyptian-Syrian co-operation. In a speech in March 1977, he termed it a "dirty alliance against Libya and against the masses in Egypt and Sudan."[46]

The food riots in Egypt in January 1977 (see survey of Egypt) were exploited to the full by Libyan anti-Sādāt propaganda. Sādāt first hinted guardedly that Libya had had a hand in the riots, and the Egyptian media soon made direct accusations to that effect. MENA, for instance, attributed to the Libyan radio "an open admission of a connection between the . . . perpetrators of the [January] subversive operations . . . on the one hand and the Libyan rulers on the other."[47] Libyan media described the measures taken in Egypt after the riots as "anti-democratic and repressive", and began calling Sādāt "a CIA agent." In an open letter to Sādāt, Qadhdhāfī said it would require "a half century of persevering strife to remove the traces" of Sādāt's "aggression on the national cause" and his "high treason"; of the "shame . . . and humiliation" of the 1975 Sinai agreement; "of massing armies" opposite Libyan villages and oases; and of launching a "campaign of starvation and mass killings" against the Egyptian people.[48]

For the first time since the previous autumn, the Egyptian government again announced the arrest of Libyan saboteurs operating in Egypt in March 1977. The Egyptian Attorney-General said that two groups had been assigned the task of carrying out sabotage acts intended to upset the course of the Arab-African summit in Cairo, from 7-9 March. (Qadhdhafī had not attended the summit and had tried to persuade Arab and African leaders to stay away as well.) Egypt reacted by stepping up its preparedness along the border: on 26 and 27 March, the War Minister, Gen Muḥammad 'Abd al-Ghanī Jamasī, inspected the Egyptian forces in the border area "with a view to intensifying their operations."[49] Egyptian troops in the area were reinforced and carried out military manoeuvres. Again, as in July 1976, Egyptian spokesmen explained that this was done to prevent further infiltration of Libyan sabotage groups into Egyptian territory. On 9 April, Libyan crowds demonstrating against Sādāt broke into the Egyptian Relations Office in Benghazi and destroyed it. (Following the establishment of the Federation of Arab Republics in 1971, the Egyptian, Syrian and Libyan embassies and consulates in the three member-states had been renamed Relations Offices.) Libyan reports claimed that the office had become "a den of espionage and terrorism." Its staff and their families were detained and, on 16 April, expelled to Egypt. In retaliation, "citizens of Alexandria" set fire to the Libyan Relations Office there the following day.

At the same time, Libyan sources frequently commented threateningly on the future of the Egyptians working in Libya. (The Libyans at that time put their number at 250,000; the Egyptians at 220,000.) The Libyan media asserted that their expulsion would hurt the Egyptian economy more than Libya's. The stoppage of their remittances would aggravate Egypt's balance of payment problems and their return to Egypt would increase unemployment there. One characteristic comment read: "Sādāt, in his behaviour, intends to oblige us to adopt a decision against them."[50] Beginning late in April, hundreds of Egyptian workers were expelled from Libya, and the issuing of new visas to Egyptian visitors and workers was suspended. However, these measures had little immediate effect on the total number of Egyptians in Libya.

Libya demanded a special session of the Arab League on 28 April to discuss the mounting tension. Egypt opposed the demand; the other Arab states took no stand, and the meeting did not take place. On the same day, *Al-Ahrām* reported that the USSR had addressed a note to a number of (unnamed) Arab capitals, saying in part: "One can clearly see the Egyptian military pressure on Libya as an attempt to stir up an armed clash", and to encourage domestic action against Qadhdhāfī's regime. Fighting actually erupted only in July (see below). It is a moot point whether the Soviet warning caused Sādāt to delay plans already laid for the spring, or whether the warning was ahead of time.

While the above developments took place in the spring and early summer of 1977, Egyptian (and, after a while, also Sudanese) statements placed increasing emphasis on Libyan collusion with the USSR. Rather than stress Libya's own subversive intentions, they now described Tripoli as the main instrument of Soviet schemes, and as the jumping-off ground for the implementation of Soviet plans directed against Arab and African countries. Egypt and Sudan were described as the primary targets against which the USSR had enlisted Libyan as well as Ethiopian support. The community of Egyptian-Sudanese interests in the face of such hostile intent was underlined in official statements as well as in the media of both countries. During his tour of Western Europe and the US in April, Sādāt repeatedly warned of Libya becoming a base for the achievement of Soviet ambitions in Africa and the Mediterranean. The fighting in southern Zaïre in April and May (in which the Egyptian air force rendered some limited assistance to Zaïre) was made an occasion to enlarge on these themes.

In June, an attempt was made at mediating between Egypt and Libya by Bashīr al-Rābitī, the Libyan speaker of the nominal parliament of the Federation of Arab Republics. Propaganda warfare was toned down for a few weeks by both sides, and Libya stopped the expulsion of Egyptians. But on 12 June, Qadhdhāfī said that Libya had not asked for mediation and considered it a "rash step." An immediate deterioration followed. Broadcasts from both sides resumed their appeals for the overthrow of the neighbouring regime in terms similar to those used a year before. On 18 July, Egypt accused Libya of support for the extreme Islamic clandestine opposition group, Jamā'at al-Takfīr wal-Hijra (for details, see survey of Egypt).

At the same time, Egypt tried, with a measure of success, to add Chad to the existing anti-Libyan combination of Egypt and Sudan. On 10 July 1977, the Egyptian Vice-President, Ḥusnī Mubārak, accompanied by the chief of staff, Gen Muḥammad 'Alī Fahmī, visited Khartoum and, together with Sudanese officials, proceeded to Chad "in the framework of arrangements against Qadhdhāfī's conspiracies" against these countries.[51] The political commentator of Libya's news agency termed Mubārak's mission "a declaration of war" against Libya.[52]

On 19 July, the first major military clash occurred along the Libyan-Egyptian border. The military initiative in the field was Egypt's but, as Egyptian statements show, Sādāt interpreted Libya's actions as intended to goad him into opening hostilities. In speeches shortly after the violence erupted, the President, Prime Minister and War Minister gave their version of the background to Egypt's action. Sādāt said: "During the past three years, Qadhdhāfī has played with fire. This madman is spending his time on subversive activity, sabotage operations and training camps."[53] Prime Minister Mamdūḥ Sālim stated that Egypt had felt threatened by the growing Soviet political and military presence in Libya. Qadhdhāfī was "conspiring in Africa against Eritrea, Somalia, Zaïre, Sudan and Chad", and was stockpiling Soviet arms "in higher quantities than he could absorb."[54] Foreign press reports spoke of sophisticated electronic surveillance systems being built by the Soviets along the Libyan border, enabling both Libya and the USSR to track Egyptian air and naval movements in Egypt itself and in the Mediterranean. The War Minister, Jamasī, elaborated on this theme: "There is a plan to throw a hostile cordon around Egypt and its strategic depth in Sudan. The planners found Libya to the east and Ethiopia to the south to be the best positions for making the cordon, and Zaïre would complete the cordon if it were to be dominated by hostile elements." Jamasī added that the plan was a Soviet one, but Libya's role in it was "consistent with its [own] aims against Egypt."[55]

Against this background armed clashes started in July 1977. According to the Egyptian account, Egyptian forces caught a group of saboteurs on their way into Egypt from a Libyan camp at the Jaghbūb oasis on 12 July. On 16 July, several Egyptian border posts were attacked by Libyan forces. On 19 July, Egyptian posts were again attacked and nine Egyptian soldiers killed. The Libyan version was that Egyptian forces had occupied positions on the Libyan side of the frontier for several months prior to the first major clashes. Some incidents had already occurred in June, when Egyptian forces raided a number of Libyan police posts and kidnapped eight Libyan policemen. The Egyptian authorities had ignored all Libyan attempts to have the men returned. In retaliation, a Libyan unit captured an Egyptian patrol numbering thirteen men on 16 July. On 17 July, the Libyan district commander warned his Egyptian counterpart that he would destroy an Egyptian position set up inside Libyan territory unless it was evacuated within two days. The Egyptians failed to withdraw and, on 19 July, the Libyans destroyed the post.

Fighting on a more massive scale began on 21 July and lasted until 24 July. Egyptian sources first described the operation on 21 July as a pre-emptive attack against a Libyan column moving towards the Egyptian border town of Salūm. Later, however, Egypt's military moves were explained as a retaliatory action for the Libyan attack two days earlier: already, on 19 July, according to Sādāt, "orders were given to repulse [Libyan] aggression." Egyptian forces accordingly entered the Libyan border townlet of Musā'id and engaged the Libyan unit sent to meet them.[56] The fighting at Musā'id remained the principal engagement of ground forces during the four days of fighting. The Egyptian forces left Libyan territory on the following morning. From 22–24 July, most fighting was done by the Egyptian air forces. Libya's Jamāl 'Abd al-Nāsir air base (formerly Al-Adem base), 30 km south of Tobruk, was bombed several times. Tobruk itself was bombed on 23 July. This was the deepest Egyptian air penetration into Libya—a distance of 120 km. Another Libyan air base, at the Kufra oasis in south-east Libya, was also heavily bombed. On 23 and 24 July, Libyan targets near the border were hit from the air. An Egyptian commando force raided a training camp in the Jaghbūb area on 24 July. Some observers, (including the *Financial Times*, 26 July), believed that the main aim of the Egyptian air attacks was to knock out Soviet-built installations along the border.

Fighting stopped on 24 July, following a series of mediation moves, chiefly by Algeria's President, Houari Boumedienne, the Kuwait Foreign Minister, Sabāḥ al-Aḥmad al-Jābir, and the PLO chairman Yāsir 'Arafāt. Sādāt, as well as his War Minister, declared that Egypt's aim had been to "teach Qadhdhāfī a lesson." Military operations were therefore on a limited scale and restricted to military targets only. They rejected the Libyan charge that, at Musā'id and elsewhere, Egyptian fire had been directed against civilians. Sādāt said that while administering a warning to Qadhdhāfī, Egypt was not hostile towards the Libyan people or armed forces. "Egypt does not want [Qadhdhāfī's] aid, money, land or anything else"; nor did it covet Libyan oil. But Sādāt went on: "Let there be no games with the armed forces . . . The lesson taught will be five times harder if even a slight encroachment on our Egyptian western border were to take place [again]. . . . I also warn against any subversive action inside this country. I can blow things up for [Qadhdhāfī] in Libya more and better." Referring indirectly, and somewhat more cautiously, to the Soviet presence in Libya, Sādāt added: "I am saying this so that Libya's brave boy will hear me—we accept neither mercenaries nor major powers in Africa nor, of course, in our Arab world . . . For this reason I warn."[57]

Following the suspension of hostilities, a relative lull set in. Propaganda warfare was again toned down to some extent and on 24 August, prisoners taken in July were exchanged through the mediation of 'Arafāt. An agreement to establish military ceasefire observation posts was concluded by means of direct contacts between the two sides.

Basic attitudes on both sides, however, remained unchanged. The Egyptian position was restated by Premier Sālim in an address to the People's Assembly (parliament). He made the following points:

1) "Egypt denounces any interference in African affairs by any [outside] state or big power.

2) "Egypt does not agree to the presence of a big international power on its border, whatever that power may be.

3) "Egypt will resolutely intervene against any attempt to dominate fraternal Sudan or the sources of the Nile, because this is a matter of life or death to Egypt."

Egypt, Sālim added, did not fear the expulsion of the Egyptian workers from Libya. They could not easily be replaced there. Should they be deported nonetheless, Egypt had worked out a contingency plan for their repatriation.[58]

Libya also reaffirmed some of its basic positions which had led to the build-up of tension prior to the July fighting. For instance, on 25 July, the Libyan newspaper *Al-Jihād* wrote: "Libya will categorically reject any so-called mediation . . . which will be aimed at putting pressure . . . on Libya in order to make it adhere to the capitulationist plans" (*vis-à-vis* the US and Israel). Libya's Prime Minister, 'Abd al-Salām Jallūd, said on 1 August that Egypt, which pretended to have handed out a lesson, had in reality been taught one by Libya. He implied that he saw no chances for a real reconciliation with the existing Egyptian regime, saying that hostile propaganda could stop if Egypt ended it first; but "no solution can be reached unless a *coup* takes place in Egypt . . . [and] unless Egypt's policy returns to the pan-Arab line."[59] The atmosphere, in the autumn of 1977, was thus one of a dispute suspended rather than resolved.

An interesting sidelight was thrown by the Libyan-Egyptian developments on the state of Syrian-Egyptian relations in mid-year. It has already been noted that Syria had not come out in support of Egypt or criticized Libya during the crisis in July. In August, after Egyptian-Syrian relations had just taken a turn for the worse (see above), a delegation of the Libyan Arab Socialist Union visited Damascus for talks with the Syrian Ba'th Party's Foreign Relations Bureau. The visit (which had not been previously announced) was stated to have dealt with "strengthening the current fraternal relations" between the Syrian Ba'th Party and the Libyan Arab Socialist Union.[60]

MAGHRIB AFFAIRS

Algeria's relations with other Arab countries were primarily determined by its dispute with Morocco and Mauritania over the issue of the Western (formerly Spanish) Sahara, and by the attitudes adopted on this question by Arab states not directly involved. (For the division of the Spanish Sahara between Morocco and Mauritania in 1976 and its antecedents, and for the roots of Algerian opposition to it and of its support for the secessionist Polisario, see *Africa Contemporary Record 1974-5*, *1975-6*, and *1976-7*.)

In 1976 and 1977, Algeria continued to support Polisario both by extending diplomatic recognition to the Saharan Arab Democratic Republic (SADR), the independent state proclaimed by Polisario, and by financial and military aid to

Polisario units enabling them to sustain, and at times escalate, their military operations in the Western Sahara. Algeria insisted on the right of self-determination by the inhabitants of the Western Sahara, thus in effect demanding a reopening of the Spanish-Moroccan-Mauritanian negotiations which had led to the division of the territory. Morocco and Mauritania, on the other hand, held that the division was final. In the words of Morocco's Foreign Minister, Aḥmad Laraki (Al-'Irāqī), during a visit to Cairo: "The case of the Sahara is closed completely . . . The Sahara has been annexed . . . for good."[61]

Algeria's main interest in inter-Arab affairs in 1976 and 1977 lay in enlisting other Arab states to support its stand on the Sahara. By and large, these efforts failed. The only country to support Algeria explicitly was Libya, predisposed to do so by an earlier quarrel of its own with Morocco, which had started in 1971. However, Libya stopped short of recognizing SADR. Some Arab countries (notably Egypt, Saudi Arabia and Tunisia) sided with Morocco and Mauritania; but the majority refused to take a stand. Attempts by Algeria to have the Western Sahara question put on the agenda of the Arab League were prevented in 1976 and 1977, mainly by the stonewalling tactics of those unwilling to adopt or declare their attitude.

Algeria repaid Qadhdhāfī for his stand by consistent support (particularly in the Algerian media, less so by official pronouncements) for Libya's line in the latter's quarrels with Egypt and Sudan (see above). Algerian efforts were instrumental in ending the Libyan-Egyptian fighting in July 1977 under circumstances not too unfavourable, politically speaking, to Libya. High-level contacts between Libya and Algeria were maintained from time to time. On 4 May 1977, on the occasion of signing a protocol envisaging economic co-operation, Libya's Premier, 'Abd al-Salām Jallūd, spoke of future "unionist steps" between the two countries; but he failed to elicit any response from Algeria.

Tunisia found itself caught in 1977 between an unfriendly Algeria and a hostile Libya. Relations with the former were strained mainly because Tunisia sided with Morocco over the Sahara; and with the latter because of a dispute over the division of the continental shelf in the Gulf of Gabès. Matters came to a head off Gabès in May 1977, when a Libyan-owned oil rig was anchored in waters claimed by Tunisia. However, Tunisia felt compelled to tread cautiously. A visit to Tunis by the Algerian Foreign Minister, 'Abd al-'Azīz Bouteflika, in February 1977 led to a slight improvement of relations with Algeria; and an agreement, concluded in June 1977 to submit the issue of the continental shelf to arbitration by the International Court of Justice, reduced the strain with Libya.

Because Algeria, as well as its Arab neighbours, were on the whole mainly concerned with the regional issues of North Africa, their impact on general Arab affairs was marginal in 1976 and 1977. That the heads of state of Morocco, Algeria, Tunisia and Libya were all absent from the 1976 Cairo summit is one indication of this fact.

Conversely, the eastern Arab world did not concern itself too much with Maghrib affairs. The exception—ineffectual at that—was a Saudi attempt in 1976 to mediate over the issue of the Western Sahara. Between 11 and 22 November 1976, the Saudi Crown Prince, accompanied by his Foreign Minister, Sa'ūd al-Faysal, held talks with King Ḥasan, President Boumedienne and the Mauritanian President, Mokhtar Ould Daddah. The failure of the talks became evident as soon as they were concluded, when King Hasan told an interviewer that Morocco agreed to a dialogue with Algeria on condition that the Moroccan and Mauritanian character of the Western Sahara would not thereby be called into question.[62]

RED SEA AFFAIRS

In 1976 and 1977, Red Sea affairs, which in the past had hardly ever been dealt with as an all-Arab issue, became a central topic at a number of inter-Arab meetings.

A short while after the 1973 war, Muḥammad Ḥasanayn Haykal (then still editor of *Al-Ahrām*) had written of the urgent need for a common Arab Red Sea strategy which would take into account the lessons of the war. However it was only in 1976 that a high level meeting took up the issue. The Sudanese Foreign Minister, Manṣūr Khālid, explained the slowness of this process: "For a while the Red Sea was a dormant issue. The Suez Canal was closed, there was no Soviet presence in the area, the sea had lost its strategic value . . . But then the Soviets established air and sea bases in the area, the Suez Canal was reopened, and trade and oil traffic increased through the Red Sea. Ethiopia has now turned towards Russia, and the danger of a Soviet-American confrontation in the area is heightened. The Arab countries bordering the Red Sea do not want . . . to allow any of the super-powers to use the area as part of their strategy. They would like the Red Sea to become a neutral zone."[63]

The first Arab meeting to take up Red Sea affairs was the Jidda conference held from 17–19 July 1976 with the participation of King Khālid and Presidents Sādāt and Numayrī. Its declared purpose was to discuss the security problem posed for Egypt and Sudan by Libyan and Soviet policies (which had caused Egypt and Sudan to conclude the defence agreement of 15 July; see above). It was President Numayrī who later revealed in an interview that the Jidda conference had discussed Red Sea affairs in general with a view to arriving at "a definition of the steps which had to be taken to maintain conformity, co-operation and co-ordination [in that area] in a well defined strategy in the service of the Arab nation." In the same interview, he stated that the Red Sea and the states bordering on it "have long constituted a natural unity."[64] On 31 October, he reiterated that the Jidda meeting had dealt with Red Sea security questions, adding that other Red Sea littorals were expected to join Egypt, Sudan and Saudi Arabia at the appropriate time. He warned of great power conflicts extending to the Red Sea and went on to say that, if Communism made gains in the region "the responsibility devolving on the Red Sea states goes beyond a limited vision."[65]

The next inter-Arab meeting to touch on Red Sea matters was King Khālid's visit to Sudan (31 October–1 November 1976). A joint communiqué stated that King Khālid and President Numayrī "affirmed their eagerness for . . . the security and peace of the Red Sea, and for working to turn it into a lake of peace for all those who live on both sides, and to keep it away from the strategies and conflicts of the super-powers."[66]

The Khartoum meeting of the presidents of Egypt, Syria and Sudan on 27–28 February 1977 (see above) included the following in its joint statement: "The Presidents affirm their desire that the Red Sea be a peace zone . . . to be kept away from international conflicts and pressures endangering the security and stability of the area. They also affirm their desire that the three countries should formulate a unified strategy in this connection and that other states in the area be invited to participate in it."[67] Similar statements were included in joint communiqués issued following frequent visits of leaders of Red Sea countries to the capitals of other littorals, or to Arab states such as the Gulf Emirates, Syria and Tunisia.

While official communiqués continued the use of phrases like "a peace zone" or "neutral region", Arab leaders frequently emphasized the "Arab character" of the Red Sea. For instance, Sādāt (December 1976): "The Red Sea is an Arab lake. This is what we think."[68] Asad (February 1977): "The Red Sea is an Arab sea."[69] Kuwait's Foreign Minister, Shaykh Sabāḥ al-Aḥmad al-Jābir (June 1977) "All the states bordering this sea are Arab states."[70]

Occasionally, a parallel was drawn between the efforts to "preserve the Arabism" of the Persian Gulf (a phrase that had come into frequent use in the late 1960s) and the status of the Red Sea. A joint statement issued on the occasion of the visit of the Sudanese Premier, Rashīd al-Tāhir Bakr, to Qatar argued that it was this similarity which made Red Sea security a "comprehensive, pan-Arab" responsibility."[71]

The principal driving force in making the Red Sea a focus of inter-Arab interest was Saudi Arabia. Its efforts were part of a general drive, dating back to the early 1970s, to rally around Saudi Arabia *first* the Arab countries along the Persian Gulf, *next* the southern part of the Arabian Peninsula, and *finally* the remaining Red Sea littorals. In keeping with its general *modus operandi* in inter-Arab affairs, Saudi leaders preferred to act behind the scenes as far as possible, concealing the broad sweep of their regional policy behind a series of bilateral meetings arranged with each of their neighbours and between other Peninsular or Red Sea states. Saudi predominance along the Arab shore of the Persian Gulf had primarily been established in 1970 and 1971. Saudi influence in North Yemen had been increasing since the end of the civil war there in 1970, and had become an established fact from the time of Lt-Col Ibrāhīm al-Ḥamdī's rise to power in 1974. In 1976, Saudi Arabia began actively to pursue a *rapprochement* with the PDRY (South Yemen), using the promise of economic assistance as the principal means to win the impoverished country over to a more pro-Saudi, less pro-Soviet, line, as well as to a greater readiness for accommodation with Oman.

South Yemen had for years supported insurgents in the southern Omani region of Dhufar in their struggle against the Sultan of Oman. Saudi Arabia did not succeed in persuading South Yemen to cut off its aid to the insurgents entirely, but border tension did abate to some extent during 1976 and 1977. Overall relations improved sufficiently by May 1976 to allow Saudi Arabia and South Yemen to establish diplomatic relations—for the first time since the latter's independence in 1967. By 1977, relations had developed further making it possible for South Yemen's Head of State, Sālim 'Alī Rubay', to visit Riyadh (31 July–2 August 1977).

Saudi Arabia extended its efforts in 1977 to bring North and South Yemen closer together. The two Heads of State met on 15–16 February in Qa'taba (North Yemen) for talks which resulted in some improvement in their relations.

Saudi Arabia's relations with Somalia have been marked by strongly ambivalent hostility. While the Saudis welcomed the non-Arab Somalis to membership of the Arab League, they strongly disapproved of the Mogadishu regime's relations with Moscow, and especially of the naval facilities afforded to the Soviet navy in Berbera. The Saudi policy was to maintain regular contacts with Somalia in an effort to get it to break its Moscow ties and draw closer to the Arab League. The chances of this happening were increased by the USSR's decision in April 1976 to court the Ethiopian military regime. The initiative to shift Somalia's policies towards the Arab world was left to the Sudan. President Numayrī undertook a mission from 15–22 March 1977 to the capitals of Oman, Somalia, South and North Yemen. This initiative led to the Ta'izz conference on 22–23 March. (Although Ethiopia was invited to attend, its regime declined to do so.) Egypt was openly involved in this move, but the Saudis remained discreetly in the background—even though the summit was specifically called to deal with the problems of the Red Sea. The countries represented by their heads of state were North and South Yemen, Sudan and Somalia. While no practical results followed from the meeting, one of its achievements was to bring together two Saudi allies and two countries hitherto hostile to it. The meeting also set a pattern for the future, and constituted an important stage in Saudi strategy for the region. The North Yemen's late Head of

State, Ibrāhīm Ḥamdī, declared that the conference was "not a demonstration against anyone . . . [nor a] plot against anyone", the participants were merely exercising their "legitimate right" to discuss "questions related to joint co-operation, including the protection of our sovereignty over our land and regional waters in the Red Sea area."[72]

According to its final communiqué, the Ta'izz meeting concentrated on aspects of economic and social co-operation. It affirmed that "the leaders agreed on the importance of exploiting the wealth of the Red Sea for the good of the peoples of the countries bordering it." A joint committee would be entrusted with continuing the efforts "to convene an expanded meeting including *all* the countries bordering on the Red Sea." There was also a brief mention of the concept of the Red Sea as a "zone of peace."[73] However, President Barreh of Somalia came away feeling that the conference had been inconclusive. He told an interviewer: "I offered to convene an enlarged conference in order to achieve a unified and comprehensive strategy for the [Red] Sea . . . but . . . in Ta'izz we achieved nothing."[74]

The Sudan's Foreign Minister went directly from Ta'izz to Riyadh to report on the discussions. Crown Prince Fahd explained: "We did not take part in any discussion regarding the security of the Red Sea or other matters, first, because we were not informed of this subject in advance and, second, because we believe that such sensitive subjects must be discussed objectively and scientifically to ascertain the objectives and dimensions of decisions taken on this matter as well as to avoid political complications that might result from them, and to ascertain the political gains that could be achieved from raising such questions. But . . . we are basically interested in the security of the Arab and Islamic world as well as the world as a whole."[75] Saudi Arabia followed up the Ta'izz meeting by sending its Foreign Minister to Somalia (5–6 April) and to Aden and San'ā (9–12 April 1977). Sa'ūd denied that a Red Sea summit had been discussed during the talks there.[76] On the occasion of the Arab League meeting in September 1977, representatives of the four states who had participated at Ta'izz, met separately and again decided to seek an enlarged Red Sea conference at which Saudi Arabia, Egypt and Jordan would participate with them. There was no immediate response to their initiative, however, and no further follow-up in fact took place up to November 1977.

A noticeable change occurred in the Red Sea policies of a number of Arab states during 1976 and 1977 with regard to Eritrea. In the past, non-littoral states—Libya, Iraq and Syria—had been among the main Arab supporters of the Eritrean liberation movement, while Egypt (because of its relations with the OAU), Sudan (because of the situation in its southern border region) and Saudi Arabia (from distaste of the supposedly revolutionary character of the Eritrean groups) had initially had strong reservations. From among the littoral states, only South Yemen had supported the Eritreans. In the wake of the change of regime in Ethiopia, especially after 1974, a policy reversal took place. Libya (pursuing its fight with Sudan which, meanwhile, had come into conflict with Ethiopia), expressed support for the Marxist regime in Addis Ababa, and ceased its earlier support for the Eritreans.

Qadhdhāfī explained Libya's policy change to a conference of Muslim Foreign Ministers in Tripoli on 16 May by saying that Libya had supported the Eritreans as long as "the feudalist reactionary agent", Haile Selassie, had ruled Ethiopia. After the revolution there, things changed. Eritrean demands for independence on religious and ethnic grounds alone were no longer valid.[77] (For rising tension along the Sudanese-Ethiopian border during this period, and for Egyptian expressions of support for Sudan, see above.) Egypt, Sudan, Saudi Arabia, Kuwait and Bahrayn now started coming to the aid of at least one of the three Eritrean groupings. After the Soviet and Cuban intervention on Ethiopia's side, South Yemen ended its support for the Eritreans. When Djibouti became an independent Republic in June 1977, it immediately joined the Arab League. President Sādāt began to speak of the countries forming the Red Sea's western shore as "Egypt, Sudan, Eritrea and Djibouti."[78]

Saudi Arabia's Crown Prince Fahd stated: "The present Ethiopian policy constitutes an open aggression against Arab nationalism. Therefore, we in the Kingdom call for co-ordination and co-operation between the Arab and Muslim states bordering the Red Sea, especially between Sudan, Somalia and the three Eritrean liberation movements. They should unite in order that a strong alignment is established to ward off the danger."[79]

The major Arab states moved much closer to a joint Red Sea policy during 1977 than at any time before. Arab consensus was not, however, complete. South Yemen, though no longer ostracized, was still something of an outsider. The Somalis, too, found much less active Arab support in their campaign in the Ogaden than they had obviously expected as members of the Arab League and as recent recruits to the Egyptian-Sudanese-Saudi anti-Soviet line. Libya had removed itself from the consensus altogether, as it had done over so many other Arab issues. Above all, Saudi Arabia would not let itself be rushed into more decisive action before it considered the time ripe in its own cautious judgement. (For a fuller discussion of the Red Sea conflict see essay on the region in this volume.)

THE ARAB LEAGUE

For most of the period reviewed, the Arab League fulfilled the role to which it had been relegated since the early 1960s: that of taking care of the routine business of Arab co-ordination over matters which did not involve major political decisions. Since 1964, it was the Arab summit conferences which had instead become the forum for major all-Arab decisions—the conclusive testing-ground for the overall state of Arab co-operation or rivalry. Since the late 1960s, and particularly since the utter failure of the Rabat summit in December 1969, it had become the practice to avoid summit meetings at times when there was no fairly broad Arab consensus on major issues, and when the success of the "meeting of Kings and Presidents" could not be considered as reasonably assured in advance. This, in turn, created the impression that any undue delay in convening a summit meeting was evidence of lack of consensus—just as much as an unsuccessful summit meeting would have been. This was particularly true of the period following the 1973 war, when a year without a summit came to be thought of in the Arab world as one of flagging Arab solidarity. The Algiers summit of 1973 had given expression to the broad (though not quite comprehensive) consensus engendered by the war; the Rabat summit of 1974 had centred on the agreement of opinion regarding the PLO (which had been in grave doubt only a few months earlier); the failure to hold a summit in 1975 had reflected the Arab disputes surrounding the second Sinai agreement of that year; the Cairo summit of October 1976 had signalled their termination.

The particular circumstances which made 1977 another year without a summit conference provide an instructive illustration of the dynamics of Arab politics. The 1976 Cairo summit, for all its importance, was soon perceived by many Arab leaders as having left too many questions open. By endorsing the Riyadh resolutions, it had disposed of the major repercussions of the Lebanese war on inter-Arab relations, and had put a stop to the Syrian-Egyptian dispute in its overt form. It had not, however, laid down a clear programme for future action. What remained unsettled were the major aspects of how to present the Arab case to the incoming US Administration; how to deal with the Palestinian issue; and how to create a binding framework for the economic aid to be provided for the "confrontation" states. As early as January 1977, Tunisia's Foreign Minister,

Ḥabīb Shattī, chairman of the routine Arab League meeting then being held, spoke of the need for a new summit conference. It should, he asserted, convene in March in conjunction with the Afro-Arab summit meeting, and should discuss "joint Arab strategy" and the future Palestinian state. However, although the Afro-Arab summit was held in Cairo (from 7-9 March 1977), his suggestion was not acted upon.

In May, North Yemen also came out with an appeal for a summit to decide on the "future Middle Eastern strategy" of the Arab states. On 15 June 1977, Libya formally took up the call, proposing as the main items on the agenda the Palestine question and the occupied territories, Arab economic co-operation and the Western Sahara. However, the venue and date proposed by Libya immediately revealed that its main purpose was to embarrass Egypt: the summit was to be held in Tripoli (where, against the background of the prevailing Egyptian-Libyan tension described above, Sādāt was unlikely to go)—and especially not on 23 July, Egypt's Revolution Day. After some equivocation by a number of Arab states, it became clear that Libya could not muster a majority for its proposal which Egypt proceeded to demolish. The Egyptian Foreign Ministry spokesman said: "The Arab Heads of State are in direct and constant contact with each other on all matters of interest to the Arab nation. It appears that there is nothing new or pressing now that merits the urgent convening of . . . [a] summit conference."[80] As Libyan-Egyptian tension rose to the point of armed hostilities in the following month, *Al-Ahrām* (20 July) recalled the Libyan suggestion, condemning it as an attempt "to plant a time bomb to shatter Arab cohesion and solidarity at this delicate, critical and fateful stage."

In the absence of a summit meeting, and under the pressure of outside events, the Arab League regained, at least for a brief moment, its former role as a forum for genuine inter-Arab discussion and decision-making. The League Council meeting, routinely set for 3 September 1977, found itself faced with the task of preparing Arab policy for the Foreign Ministers' talks with the US Administration and for the UN General Assembly, both scheduled to open later the same month. As noted above, the meeting brought Syrian-Egyptian policy differences into the open again. But the controversy also touched on the question of convening a summit: Syria demanded that a summit be held on October, i.e. at a time when its decisions would still have a bearing on Arab conduct at the UN, and on major developments in the Arab-Israeli conflict which were then thought to be imminent. Egypt was unwilling to let a summit convene at a time when its deliberations were likely to reflect, perhaps even to underline Syrian-Egyptian differences, and when there was no telling which of the two would command a majority at a summit meeting. At Egypt's insistence (and with the support of Saudi Arabia, who backed Egypt on every issue during the September League session) the Council decided to set an Arab Foreign Ministers' meeting for 12 November 1977. This meeting would in turn set a date, agree on a venue and draw up an agenda for the summit. The League's Secretary-General, Maḥmūd Riyāḍ, said that by November the Arab countries would have had time for "intensive contacts to clear the Arab atmosphere."[81] However, a preparatory meeting so late in the year made it almost certain that 1977 would pass without a summit.

A year after the 1976 Cairo summit, its main achievements were thus being called into question. In September 1977, Syria and Egypt were not pulling in the same direction; Saudi Arabia (much against its inclination and basic policy) had been forced to take sides in favour of Egypt; and the year would run out without that reaffirmation of Arab solidarity which a new summit was to have signified.

NOTES

1. Radio Cairo and Radio Damascus, 18 October—monitored by Daily Report, East and North Africa (DR), 19 October; and British Broadcasting Corporation Summary of World Broadcasts, the ME and Africa (BBC), 20, 21 October 1976.
2. R Damascus, 5 October; R Cairo, 6 October—BBC, 7, 8 October 1976.
3. *Newsweek*, 5 January 1976.
4. Middle East News Agency (MENA), 20 October—DR, 20 October 1976.
5. Iraqi News Agency (INA), 25 October—DR, 26 October 1976.
6. *Al-Sayyād*, Beirut; according to MENA, 30 December 1976.
7. *Al-Anwār*, Beirut; in a series published 20-23 May 1977.
8. R Cairo, 11, 17 December—DR, 13, 20 December 1976.
9. MENA, 11 January—DR, 12 January 1977. *Le Monde*, 21 January 1977.
10. R Cairo and R Damascus, 21 December—BBC, 23 December 1976.
11. MENA, 11 January—DR, 12 January 1977.
12. *Al-Akhbār*, Cairo; 9 May—DR, 11 May 1977.
13. R Damascus, 4 August—BBC, 6 August 1977.
14. R Damascus, 9 August—BBC, 11 August 1977.
15. *Al-Ba'th*, Damascus; quoted by Syrian Arab News Agency (SANA), 7 August—BBC, 9 August 1977.
16. See *Al-Siyāsa*, Kuwait; 13 August 1976.
17. R Amman, 22 November—BBC, 24 November 1976.
18. R Amman, 8 December—BBC, 10 December 1976.
19. R Amman, 19 January—BBC, 21 January 1977.
20. *Al-Akhbār*, 23 February 1977.
21. R Amman, 3 July—BBC Weekly, 12 July 1977.
22. *Newsweek*, 1 August 1977.
23. MENA, 14 January; R Amman, 14, 15 January—DR, 17 January 1977. *Al-Ra'y*, Amman; 16 January 1977.
24. R Amman, 20 January—BBC, 22 January 1977.
25. *Ākhir Sā'a*, Cairo; 19 January—DR, 25 January 1977.
26. *Jordan Times*, 12 July 1977.
27. MENA, 10 July—DR, 11 July 1977.
28. R Riyadh—DR, 24 March 1977.
29. R Riyadh, 19 May—BBC, 21 May 1977.
30. MENA, R Cairo, 19 May—DR, 20 May 1977.
31. *Al-Ḥawādith*, Beirut; 3 December 1976.
32. *Al-Siyāsa*, 16 April 1977
33. Statement by the Syrian Ba'th National Command; R Damascus, 7 March—BBC, 9 March 1977.
34. R Damascus, 22 February—BBC, 24 February 1977.
35. R Damascus, 28 March—DR, 30 March 1977.
36. R Damascus, 4 January—DR, 5 January; *Tishrīn*, 5 January; *Al-Ba'th*, 7 June 1977.
37. *Al-Thawra*, Damascus; 22 March 1977.
38. R Damascus, 5 September—BBC, 6 September 1977.
39. INA, 16 July—BBC, 18 July 1977.
40. R Cairo, 5 July; Arab Revolutionary News Agency (ARNA), Libya; 23 July—BBC, 7 July, 26 July 1976.
41. R Tripoli, 24 July—DR, 26 July 1976.
42. R Tripoli, 2 September—DR, 3 September 1976.
43. For instance, *Al-Siyāsa*, 14 August; press conference in Oman—MENA, 15 August; DR, 17 August 1976.
44. MENA, 11 January—DR, 12 January 1977.
45. R Cairo, R Damascus, 28 February—BBC, 2 March 1977.
46. ARNA, 9 March—BBC, 10 March 1977.
47. MENA, 12 February—DR, 14 February 1977.
48. ARNA, 5 February—BBC, 7 February 1977.
49. MENA, 27 March—BBC, 29 March 1977.
50. ARNA, 20 April, 29 April—BBC, 22 April; DR, 2 May. R Tripoli, 27 April—DR, 28 April 1977.
51. *Al-Ahrām*, Cairo; 12 July 1977.
52. R Tripoli, 11 July—DR, 12 July 1977.
53. R Cairo, 22 July—DR, 25 July 1977.
54. R Cairo, 2 August—DR, 3 August 1977.
55. MENA, 2 August—DR, 3 August 1977.
56. Sādāt in a speech at Alexandria University; R Cairo, 26 July—BBC, 28 July 1977.

57. R Cairo, 22 and 26 July—DR, 25 July; BBC, 28 July 1977. R Cairo, 7 August—BBC, 9 August 1977.
58. R Cairo, 2 August—DR, 3 August 1977.
59. ARNA, 2 August—DR, 2 August 1977.
60. SANA, 10 August—DR, 11 August 1977.
61. *Al-Ahrām*, 16 February 1977.
62. *Le Matin*, 22 November 1976.
63. *Events*, 6 May 1977.
64. *Al-Yamāma*, Saudi Arabia; quoted by R Omdurman, 15 October—BBC, 20 October 1976.
65. *Al-Saḥāfa*, Sudan; 2 November 1976.
66. R Riyadh, 1 November—BBC, 3 November 1976.
67. MENA, 28 February—DR, 1 March 1977.
68. Interview to *al-Sayyād*, quoted by MENA, 30 December 1976—DR, 4 January 1977.
69. Press conference after the Khartoum conference; MENA, 28 February—DR, 1 March 1977.
70. MENA, 25 June—DR, 27 June 1977.
71. Qatari News Agency, 16 May—DR, 17 May 1977.
72. R San'ā, 22 March—BBC, 24 March 1977.
73. R San'ā, 23 March—BBC, 25 March 1977.
74. *Al-Jumhūriyya*, Cairo; 12 May 1977.
75. Interview with *al-Siyāsa*, 16 April 1977.
76. *Al-Bilād*, Jidda; quoted by R Riyadh, 20 April—DR, 21 April 1977.
77. ARNA, 16 May—DR, 17 May 1977.
78. Interview with an Iranian correspondent; quoted by MENA, 18 May—DR, 19 May 1977.
79. Interview with *al-Anwār*, 21 May 1977.
80. R Cairo, 19 June—DR, 20 June 1977.
81. MENA, 4 September 1977.

The Palestine Liberation Organization

ISRAEL ALTMAN

Developments in the Palestine Liberation Organization (PLO) from the latter part of 1976 to the middle of 1977 should be seen against the background of the chain of events starting with the Arab-Israeli war in October 1973, and culminating in the ceasefire in the civil war in Lebanon three years later. The major developments during that period were: 1) a consistent improvement in the PLO's international standing contrasting with a decline, from 1975 onwards, in its position in the Arab world; 2) increasing pressures, external and internal, on the PLO to participate in the political process towards a Middle Eastern settlement, leading to some modification of positions which resulted in internal conflict; and 3) the political and military effects wrought by the civil war in Lebanon.

Arab diplomacy following the October 1973 war produced ever-widening recognition of the PLO. This process was highlighted by the Rabat summit conference resolution recognizing the PLO as the "sole legitimate representative of the Palestinian people" (28 October 1974), followed by PLO Executive Committee Chairman Yāsir 'Arafāt's appearance at the UN and the adoption by the General Assembly of Resolution 3236 (22 November 1974), affirming the Palestinian people's right to national independence and self-determination.

However, developments in the political process raised apprehensions within the PLO of a possible ME settlement being arrived at without its active participation, and in which its own aspirations would not be fully taken into account. In order to affirm its position as a partner to any settlement, the PLO found itself faced with the need to modify some of its traditional positions, such as agreeing to Palestinian sovereignty over *part* of Palestine (thereby possibly jeopardizing its claim to the entire area of Palestine). There was also a growing recognition by PLO leaders of the need felt by many Palestinians to reinforce their Palestinian identity, politically and legally, through the actual creation of a Palestinian state.

Lacking a territorial base of its own independent from any host government, the PLO's ideological stand—as the "spearhead" and symbol of pan-Arab commitment to the total liberation of Palestine—had been its major political asset. In the wake of the 1973 war, internal disputes evolved around the question of the legitimacy of deviating from ideological positions which until then were considered to be absolute. Those who opposed any deviation whatsoever formed the Palestinian "Rejection Front" in the autumn of 1974. The PLO leadership (i.e. its central establishment, largely dominated by al-Fatḥ) strove instead to preserve its basic ideological stand, and yet modify certain positions by introducing a distinction between "strategic" and "tactical" goals. "Strategic" goals were those sanctioned by official ideology (embodied in the Palestinian National Covenant); "tactical" goals were dictated by circumstances at a given juncture. The latter were held to be legitimate because they were intended, and perceived, as steps towards the realization of the "strategic" goals.

The second Sinai disengagement agreement in 1975 led the PLO into political conflict with Egypt. In 1976, the PLO's efforts to secure a truly autonomous foothold in Lebanon brought it into military conflict with Syria, formerly its closest ally. The war damaged the PLO's position in the Arab world, and enabled Syria and Jordan to undermine its claim to exclusive representation of the Palestinians. As a result of the war, the PLO's freedom of military movement and action was much more circumscribed by Syria. Yet the hostilities probably improved the organization's ability to handle its combat units more effectively and on a larger scale than before.

The main division inside the PLO—between the Rejection Front and al-Fatḥ—was temporarily bridged during the war, with both sides ranged against the "common enemy": Syria and the pro-Syrian elements in the PLO, chiefly al-Sāʻiqa (an organization actually run by Syria).

The PLO's defeats in Lebanon did not diminish international recognition of its role in negotiations for a Middle East settlement. On the contrary, support grew in the US and Western Europe for PLO participation in the negotiating process.

INTERNAL DEVELOPMENTS IN THE PLO

The central issue in internal PLO affairs in 1977 was again the question of its participation in "the political process" towards finding a settlement to the ME conflict, and the modifications it might have to make in its policies to gain a place in that process. This question had been crucial in 1974, but had been pushed into the background in the latter part of 1975 and in 1976 by issues stemming from the PLO's involvement in the Lebanese war.

In the autumn of 1974, four PLO member organizations had formed a coalition to fight what they perceived as the willingness of al-Fatḥ, the largest and leading group in the PLO (as well as of al-Sāʻiqa and the Popular Democratic Front for the Liberation of Palestine, PDFLP, led by Nā'if Ḥawātima) to accept in principle a political settlement to the ME conflict and to the Palestinian question. The coalition called itself "The Front of Palestinian Forces Rejecting Capitulationist Settlements [to the conflict]", or more popularly, "the Rejection Front." It consisted of the Popular Front for the Liberation of Palestine (PFLP, led by Dr George Ḥabash), the Popular Front for the Liberation of Palestine-General Command (PFLP-GC, led by Aḥmad Jibrīl), the pro-Iraqi Arab Liberation Front (ALF, then led by Dr ʻAbd al-Wahhāb al-Kayyālī), and the Popular Struggle Front (PSF, led by Dr Samīr Ghosha). It was supported most strongly by Libya, Iraq and by some of the other Arab governments whose interest in a rapid political solution to the problem of the territories occupied in June 1967 was not as acute as those which had actually suffered territorial losses.

The Rejection Front argued that under the prevailing global and regional balance of power, a political settlement would of necessity involve territorial and other concessions such as no Palestinian had the right to make. The only legitimate way to regain Palestine, it maintained, was through armed struggle. It demanded organizational changes in the PLO calculated to increase its strength in the Palestinian National Council (PNC) in relation to al-Fath. To avoid taking part in what they described as the PLO leadership's drift towards a political settlement, the Rejectionists suspended their participation in the Executive Committee (EC) in the autumn of 1974. The EC is the PLO's highest executive body and is responsible for carrying out the resolutions and recommendations adopted by the quasi-parliamentary PNC, its highest policy-making institution. The Rejectionists also suspended their participation in the Palestinian Central Council (CC), a smaller forum of PNC members authorized to lay down policies on issues of crucial and immediate importance between regular PNC sessions.

However, the Rejectionist groups did not withdraw from the PNC itself. Anxious to avoid having its authority and power challenged, the Fatḥ-dominated EC continuously delayed reconvening the PNC, despite the repeated and constitutionally well-founded calls by the Rejectionists to do so. [In the PLO Fundamental Statute (*al-niẓām al-asāsī*) of 1964, the PNC's term of office was set at three years. Originally, it was to meet once a year; but following a 1968 amendment, once every six months. The fourth PNC had been formed in 1971 and had last convened in June 1974 (for the 12th PNC session held since its establishment in 1964). The term of office of the fourth PNC had expired in July 1974. Nevertheless, a new (fifth) PNC was neither formed nor convened until March 1977.]

In late 1976 and early 1977, the PLO leadership came under pressure from Arab countries (notably Egypt and Saudi Arabia) to reconvene the PNC in the expectation that its resolutions would be helpful to the "political process." There were also Syrian pressures on the PLO to enlarge the membership of the PNC and to change the balance of power—to Syria's advantage—by adding a large number of delegates who were not members of any one of the PLO's constituent fidā'ī organizations. Syria's intention was to weaken al-Fath's hold on the PNC, so as to prevent a censure of Syria's role in Lebanon during the war; to obtain a tacit legitimization of the Syrian presence there after the war's termination; to ensure the rehabilitation of al-Sā'iqa; and to secure PLO co-operation in implementing the Cairo agreement in Lebanon (see section on the PLO's relations with Syria). It should be noted that the PNC is not an elected body: its delegates are selected by a committee, dominated in fact by the incumbent EC. The selection involves a complicated bargaining process. Hence it was possible for Syria to use its influence to try and change the PNC's size and composition.

When the selection committee completed its work in February 1977, the membership of the fifth PNC was indeed larger than before—289 instead of 187. Nonetheless, al-Fatḥ managed to preserve its dominance.

The newly formed PNC met in Cairo from 12–20 March 1977 for its thirteenth session. Compared to the 12 to 18 preceding months, the session was characterized by the shifts it reflected in PLO alliances and internal conflicts. The open conflict which, during the Lebanese war, had ranged al-Sā'iqa against the rest of the Palestinian organizations (except Ahmad Jibrīl's faction of the PFLP-GC; see below) had gradually subsided, leaving the Rejection Front again pitted against the PLO leadership. Nevertheless, the March session achieved a degree of understanding between the two sides, most significantly on the issue of the setting up of a Palestinian state in a part of Palestine.

That understanding was facilitated by the Rejection Front's general weakening, following its heavy losses in Lebanon, and the relative decline in the influence that its main backers—Libya and Iraq—had in the region (see essay on inter-Arab relations). The PLO leadership, for its part, was willing to see the PNC session adopt a resolution tough enough to be accepted by the majority of Rejectionist delegates. In exchange, the PLO leadership under Yāsir 'Arafāt was given considerable latitude to negotiate on behalf of the PLO. This was apparent in the PNC's Political Declaration, unopposed by most of the Rejectionist delegates, which avoided an explicit rejection of PLO participation in Geneva. (For text of the Declaration, see Appendix 1).

It is likely that some form of advance agreement had been reached between al-Fath and the Rejection Front leaders on the final PNC political statement. Some reports went so far as to assert that an advance agreement had been reached "on all aspects of the PNC session, as well as on all the important organizational issues in the PLO."[1] They suggested that a political working document, signed by all groups and factions, was to be presented for the PNC's approval. A "secret circular" on the PNC session (ascribed to al-Fath), claimed that the Rejection Front and al-Fath leaders had reached an agreement on the Political Declaration in order to allow the

PLO to emerge from the session with a united Palestinian stand. To make this possible, every faction was asked to put its reservations to any of the Declaration's articles in writing to the PNC chairman so that they would be on record.[2]

Eventually, from among the c. 70 Rejection Front delegates at the PNC (namely, members of the "rejectionist" organizations as well as "independents" affiliated with them), only the 12 PFLP representatives and the one delegate of the pro-Iraqi faction of the PFLP-GC voted against the Political Declaration submitted by the PLO leadership; the others either supported the Declaration or abstained. Voting results were 194 for, 13 against and 82 abstentions.

The PFLP dropped its opposition to the establishment of a Palestinian state in only a part of the territory of Palestine, on the understanding that this would be the first step towards "total liberation." Yet it did not change its positions on two other, no less central, issues. It continued to reject PLO participation in the Geneva conference, arguing that the establishment of a state even in a part of Palestine must be brought about through military rather than political means; and it reaffirmed its opposition to PLO ties with Jordan, or even a dialogue with it in any form. The PFLP voted against the Political Declaration because it contained no clear rejection of PLO participation in Geneva and failed to make any reference to the PLO's hostile position regarding Jordan. Furthermore, it criticized the Declaration for its failure to denounce the contacts PLO officers had held with Israeli and pro-Zionist personalities and groups. (For the internal debate over this issue, see below.) The pro-Iraqi faction of the PFLP-GC criticized the Declaration for the same reasons as did the PFLP, but objected to one additional point: its failure to denounce the Syrian intervention in Lebanon.

The nine ALF delegates voted for the Declaration, along with the seven delegates of Aḥmad Jibrīl's faction of the PFLP-GC. Both groups also joined the new EC (formed on 20 March 1977) and the new CC (first convened on 1 May 1977), having boycotted those institutions since the autumn of 1974. The ALF made a point of stressing that its renewed participation in the EC did not reflect a change in its rejectionist attitude; did not contradict its being a member of the Rejection Front; and was, moreover, the "result of consultations held with comrades in the Rejectionist Front who had given their approval."[3] The ALF justified its support of the Political Declaration and its joining the EC and the CC by referring to its "realization of the gravity of the conspiracy menacing the Palestine Revolution" and stressing its "concern for toughening the stands confronting this conspiracy, foiling the imperialist onslaught and thwarting the plans for the capitulationist settlement . . ., all of which would only be achieved through national unity."[4]

An additional ALF consideration was probably that avenues for the pursuit of its political objectives were wider inside the PLO's governing bodies than outside them. The fact that the PNC had not met for three years may have convinced the ALF that participation in that body alone could not give it much of a say in PLO decision-making. A similar consideration seems to have motivated the PFLP's decision to join the new CC though, unlike the ALF, it did not join the new EC.

The Rejectionist organizations' interest in furthering their relations with the main PLO leadership was to some extent related to the situation in Lebanon. Rejectionist groups were at that time engaged intermittently in armed clashes with Syrian, or pro-Syrian Palestinian, forces. In February 1977, for example, the PLO leadership helped prevent a Syrian onslaught on the PFLP, which was believed to be imminent. To this motivation should be added an interest in strengthening the overall authority of the PLO leadership in the face of Syrian pressures.

The co-operation stopped short, however, of significantly increasing Yasir 'Arafāt's personal authority. A proposal to the effect that 'Arafat should be authorized to appoint the members of the new EC failed to receive the required two-thirds of PNC votes, due to Rejection Front opposition. The new EC was therefore elected by the PNC, as had been the practice hitherto. (For the EC's composition, see Appendix 2).

In 1977, as in previous years, internal developments in the PLO were determined not only by the evolution of the ME conflict, but also by developments in two other spheres: the PLO's relations with individual Arab states, and the state of inter-Arab affairs. The on-going debate in 1977 within the PLO on the issue of its relations with Syria exemplifies the former; the manifestations of the Syrian-Iraqi dispute in conflicts within the PLO, which had started earlier but continued in 1977, serves as an example of the latter.

During the civil war in Lebanon, al-Sā'iqa (being in effect, a branch of the Syrian Ba'th party) fought alongside the Syrian forces against other Palestinian organizations. Consequently, it was for all intents and purposes disqualified by the PLO as an authentic Palestinian organization. Its leader, Zuhayr Muḥsin (who was also a member of the Syrian Ba'th National Command), was dismissed by the PLO leadership from his post as the head of the PLO Military Department.

Following the end of the war in October 1976, PLO-Sā'iqa tensions gradually subsided, though the continued use of al-Sā'iqa by Syria to promote the latter's objectives in Lebanon led to violent clashes between Fatḥ and Sā'iqa forces in December 1976 in Tripoli, Beirut and southern Lebanon. A reconciliation with al-Sā'iqa was virtually forced on al-Fatḥ by Syria at a CC meeting in Damascus in December 1976, following which Zuhayr Muḥsin was reinstated in his PLO post. Al-Sā'iqa's rehabilitation was informally sanctioned by its participation in the March 1977 PNC session.

Yet that development did not terminate the basic dispute between al-Fath and al-Sā'iqa, which forms part of the perennial debate within the PLO concerning its relations with Arab states. Al-Fath has constantly striven to assert the distinctiveness of the Palestinian identity, and to secure maximum independence of Palestinian decision-making and freedom of action, even though some of its leading personalities have acknowledged the existence of special ties with Syria. For instance, Hānī al-Ḥasan, one of 'Arafāt's associates, was quoted as saying, in July 1977 that Syrian-Palestinian relations were becoming closer "thanks to the historic relationships within the Syrian group of nations, of which Palestine is the southern part."[5]

Al-Sā'iqa, on the other hand, rejected the idea of a distinctive Palestinian nationalism, regarding Palestinian and Syrian interests as identical. In an interview given while the PNC was in session, Zuhayr Muḥsin told a Dutch paper: "Between Jordanians, Palestinians, Syrians and Lebanese there are no differences. We are part of one people, the Arab nation . . . Only for political reasons do we subscribe to our Palestinian identity."

Muḥsin went on to explain that, in his view, Palestinian nationalism was a matter of expediency: "It is, in fact, a national interest for the Arabs to encourage the existence of the Palestinians *vis-à-vis* Zionism. Yes, the existence of a separate Palestinian identity is being kept up only for tactical reasons. The establishment of a Palestinian state is a new means to continue the struggle against Israel and for Arab unity." Regarding PLO-Syrian relations, Muḥsin's view was that "the Palestinians must work together with Syria in the first place, and only after that with the other Arab states. Only Syria can play an important part in the fight against Israel."[6] Syria's supporters in the PLO also came out in favour of the Syrian position on PLO-Jordanian relations (see below).

In 1977, as in 1976, the Syrian-Iraqi conflict was acted out by proxy by Palestinian organizations in Lebanon. The split that took place in the PFLP-GC was also a reflection of Syrian-Iraqi rivalry. The ideological roots of that split go back to the 12th PNC session in June 1974, and to the question of the PFLP-GC's position on the ten-point political programme adopted by it. The secretary-general of the PFLP-GC, Ahmad Jibrīl, supported the programme, while the organization's Central Council opposed it. Jibrīl's opponents, led by Abū al-'Abbās, later succeeded in making the organization join the Rejection Front.

Following the Syrian invasion of Lebanon, the internal dispute developed into an open split. Jibrīl's opponents announced his expulsion from the organization, on the ground of his having co-operated with the Syrians.[7] Jibrīl retorted by denouncing Abū al-'Abbās and his supporters as Iraqi Intelligence Service agents.[8] Meanwhile, the two factions, each claiming to be the real PFLP-GC, clashed with each other—first in the refugee camps in the Beirut area, then in southern Lebanon. An attempted reconciliation by PLO leaders late in November 1976 failed to put a stop to the fighting.

On 23 April 1977, an agreement was reached through 'Arafāt's intervention. Aḥmad Jibrīl's faction was to retain the name PFLP-GC, whereas their rivals were given the name Palestine Liberation Front (PLF). (This had been the name of Aḥmad Jibrīl's original organization until 1967.) By assigning the two factions two different names, the PLO in effect recognized the existence of two separate organizations. Jibrīl and his group were ousted from the Rejection Front, while Abū al-'Abbās' group was admitted as a member.[9]

The Syrian-Iraqi conflict was also at the roots of the clashes that occurred during the period under review between al-Sā'iqa (sometimes aided by Syrian troops of the Arab Deterrent Force, as well as by Aḥmad Jibrīl's group) and Rejection Front units in southern Lebanon. Because of Israel's objection to the proximity of Syrian soldiers to her borders, Syria made use of pro-Syrian Palestinians to achieve her objectives in these areas. Al-Sā'iqa was also used to establish an indirect Syrian presence inside the refugee camps in Lebanon. For this purpose, al-Sā'iqa's membership was considerably expanded. This led to some tension with al-Fath in December 1976.

THE PLO IN THE ARAB-ISRAELI CONFLICT: POSITIONS, STRATEGIES AND TACTICS

Palestinian operations against Israeli targets were at an ebb during the greater part of the period reviewed. This was caused partly by operational difficulties resulting from the PLO's situation in Lebanon, and partly by its efforts to start a dialogue with the US, which would be facilitated by projecting an image of moderation and respectability. In March 1977, the PNC did admittedly resolve "to continue the armed struggle" and "to escalate the armed struggle in the occupied territory."[10] The change of government in Israel was also followed by increased terrorist activity (mainly the placing of explosives in public places, such as open air markets, shopping centres or bus stations). Yet the main PLO activity during the period was in the political-diplomatic field.

The attitudes on the ME conflict of the dominant elements in al-Fatḥ and the PLO in general (led by Yāsir 'Arafāt) were the outcome of the following principal considerations. On the one hand, it was argued that a serious attempt to reach a political solution to the ME conflict was likely to be made. In this case, the need for participation was increasingly acknowledged, on the premise that once the PLO was recognized as an equal party, it would be able either to play an active role in a settlement which satisfied its aspirations, or torpedo any solution which did not. The advocates of participation in the political process therefore found it advisable for the PLO to project an image of moderation in the conflict to facilitate its widest possible acceptance as an equal party to the settlement. The countervailing argument was that the success of the political process, even the mere reconvening of the

Geneva conference, was far from certain. Ideological concessions made in order to facilitate the PLO's acceptance as an equal party might thus very well prove valueless. Hence the reluctance on the part of the PLO leaders to endorse modifications in their basic stance on crucial issues, such as the recognition of Israel's right to exist.

The PLO's desire to secure a role in the political process, while simultaneously adhering to its established ideological position, resulted in the emergence of the "phased strategy" concept. The PLO would consent to the setting up of a Palestinian state in the West Bank and the Gaza Strip, though not in exchange for recognition of, or for ending the war with, Israel, and only as a first step towards the eventual realization of the ultimate "strategic" goal—the "liberation of Palestine" in its entirety. Similarly, the PLO demanded the right to attend the Geneva conference (or any other international forum dealing with the ME conflict), but not on the basis of Security Council Resolution 242.[11]

The "phased struggle" concept envisaged first, the establishment of a West Bank/Gaza Strip state alongside Israel in pre-1967 boundaries; second, another compression of Israel's size to boundaries laid down in the 1947 Partition Plan; and third, the establishment of a democratic, secular Palestinian state to replace Israel and to extend to the entire area of Palestine.[12]

The adherents of this concept distinguished between tactical or temporary (*marḥalī*) as opposed to strategic or permanent (*dā'im*) solutions to the Palestine problem: "The permanent solution can be realized only through the establishment of a democratic Palestinian state where Muslims, Christians and Jews will live in equality. The permanent peace is [an outcome of] the establishment of that state. This is a long-term goal. The temporary peace rests on the establishment of a Palestinian state on a part of our land."[13]

The assessment that the PLO might gain by taking its place in the political process, as well as the fear that its interests might otherwise be ignored by the Arab states and the great powers, were already reflected in the June 1974 session of the PNC. At that time, the PNC called for the setting up of an "independent fighting national authority on any part of the Palestinian territory to be liberated." The choice of the term "authority" (*sulta*), meaning a temporary or provisional body (the word "state" would have implied permanency), was to convey its purely tactical nature. This was made clear by the rest of the resolution, which stated that after its establishment "the Palestinian national authority will work to unify the confrontation states in order to complete the liberation of all the Palestinian territory . . . All liberating steps will be taken for the purpose of the continuation of the implementation of the PLO's strategy to set up a democratic Palestinian state."

Justification of the "tactical goal" by the PNC had met with strong opposition in 1974. By 1977, however, there already existed a wide acceptance not merely of an "authority", but of a *state* in the West Bank and Gaza. On 14 December 1976, the CC approved a policy favouring the setting up of a Palestinian state under the PLO in the two areas named.[14] In March 1977, the PNC resolved "to continue the struggle to regain the national rights of our people, in particular their rights of return, self-determination and establishing an independent national *state* on their national soil."[15] That decision did not define the territorial extent of the future state, but PLO spokesmen explained that the reference was to the West Bank and Gaza Strip. A territorial and aerial corridor under Palestinian sovereignty was to connect the two areas. An official territorial definition had been avoided to prevent the possible impression that the resolution was tantamount to relinquishing the "strategic" goal, namely the total liberation of Palestine.

The PNC's Political Declaration made no reference to the democratic, secular

Palestinian state to replace Israel. Yet its less publicized (but no less binding) Final Statement read: "The PNC asserts that it adheres to the PLO strategic objective to liberate Palestine . . . so that it will become a home for the Palestinian people where the democratic state of Palestine will be established."[16]

The main argument raised by Rejectionist spokesmen against the West Bank/Gaza state was that its establishment through the political process would necessarily imply recognition of Israel. PLO leaders therefore made every effort to assert that even after a Palestinian state was established on parts of Palestine, the PLO would not recognize Israel, and would use the new state to continue its struggle against her.[17] In March 1977, the PNC itself declared its decision to work for the liberation of all the occupied Arab areas without any conciliation (*sulḥ*) with, or recognition of, Israel.[18] Nevertheless, PLO leaders implied on occasions that the establishment of a Palestinian state on parts of Palestine might be followed by a period of truce between that state and Israel, though not by recognition of the latter.[19]

A document published by a Lebanese daily—described as the PLO's settlement plan submitted to the US—also implied that following the establishment of the Palestinian state, the struggle to realize Palestinian objectives would continue, even though peaceful, rather than military, means would then be employed. The state's armaments might possibly be limited in proportion to its defensive needs, thus excluding ground-to-ground and ground-to-air missile systems. No reference was made in the document to PLO recognition of Israel, but termination of PLO guerrilla warfare was offered in exchange for Israel's recognition of the PLO.[20]

Another development in PLO attitudes was the formal proclamation of its demand to participate in the Geneva conference, though on its own terms. Formerly the PLO had not shown readiness to participate in the conference. Instead, it had sought to transfer the political struggle from Geneva to the UN. In the winter of 1976–77, a shift of emphasis occurred. Rather than reject the idea of PLO participation in the conference, it now rejected Security Council Resolution 242 (and 338) as the basis for its participation. Once these were amended, or replaced, it would insist on its right to participate. Accordingly, in Point 15 of the March 1977 Political Declaration, the PNC "confirms its wish for the PLO's right to participate independently and on equal footing in all the conferences and international forums concerned with the Palestinian issue and the Arab-Zionist conflict, with a view to achieve our inalienable national rights as approved by the UN General Assembly in 1974, namely in Resolution 3236." The same shift was reflected in the PNC's abstention, in 1977, from any negative reference to the Geneva conference—in contrast with its resolutions of June 1974.

The PLO's rejection of 242 was based on the argument that the resolution referred to the problems of the territories occupied in 1967 only, and was irrelevant to the results of the 1948 war, and to the overall problems of the Palestinians which were created at that time. Consequently, Resolution 242 interpreted the issue of the Palestinians as a refugee problem only, rather than as a political one of a people demanding self-determination and statehood. Another argument was that participation at Geneva on the basis of Resolution 242 would signify recognition both of Israel's right to exist and of her pre-1967 boundaries.

Consequently, the PLO demanded that the UN General Assembly Resolution 3236 of 22 November 1974 be made the basis of the Geneva conference instead. Resolution 3236 reaffirmed the "inalienable rights" of the Palestinian people "in Palestine" (i.e. without a reference to a territorial delimitation), listing them as the right to self-determination, national independence and sovereignty, as well as the right of Palestinians "to return to their homes and property from which they have been displaced."

Furthermore, PLO spokesmen made its participation in Geneva conditional on an invitation being addressed to the PLO and signed by both the US and the USSR as co-chairmen of the conference; on PLO attendance from the beginning; on its participation in *all* the conference activities; and on the Palestine question being made a separate item on the agenda.[21] These demands reflected the PLO's suspicion that either an overall or a partial settlement might be reached by other participants at the expense of its own interests.

A possible sequel to the PLO's demand to be invited to Geneva and to establish a West Bank/Gaza state might have been a decision to form a government-in-exile or a provisional government, to represent the organization at Geneva and to prepare for the establishment of the Palestinian state. The PLO was indeed urged to set up such a government by Arab and other countries—in particular by President Sādāt and the Egyptian media.[22] According to Arab press reports, the prolonged discussions held in PLO bodies on this issue late in 1976 and early in 1977 eventually led to a decision in principle to form a provisional government, the remaining question being one of appropriate timing.[23]

Fārūq Qaddūmī was quoted as saying that "we have begun the process of creating a Palestinian entity in exile."[24] But the PNC, which had been widely expected to take the matter up,[25] did not adopt a resolution on this issue. By the end of the period reviewed, no decision to set up a government had been taken. Presumably, the PLO preferred the establishment of a provisional government on even a limited area of "liberated territory", than a government-in-exile. "It is not yet time to establish such a government", said Fārūq Qaddūmī. "We need a land on which to build our economic, political, military and cultural institutions."[26]

Dr 'Isām Sartāwī (member of al-Fatḥ's Revolutionary Council) submitted a statement of PLO positions on the Palestinian problem on 26 January 1977 to the Austrian Chancellor, Bruno Kreisky, in his capacity as chairman of the Socialist International fact-finding mission on the Middle East. The document called for the establishment of a Palestinian state in the West Bank, the Gaza Strip, and the areas of Ḥamma and 'Awja; it asserted that "between the future sovereign state of Palestine and the state of Israel, a non-belligerent status could be established." The document also spoke of a "complete state of peace" between the two states, conditional mainly on Israel's recognition, and implementation, of the right of the Palestinian refugees to return to their homes or to receive compensation.[27]

This document could, on the face of it, have signalled a significant development. It could have been viewed as implying PLO recognition of Israel's right to statehood within frontiers smaller than her pre-1967 lines, yet larger than those of the 1947 Partition Plan. It was, however, emphatically disavowed by senior PLO officials. Fārūq Qaddūmī stated that Sartāwī "absolutely did not submit a document to Kreisky, nor did he speak on behalf of the PLO. He merely submitted a letter containing ideas in his personal capacity."[28] There was no way of knowing what weight to attach to Sartāwī's "personal" ideas.

Prior to the ordinary session of PNC in March 1977, it was expected that the Council would amend the Palestinian National Covenant (drawn up in 1964, amended in 1968). There were several Palestinian statements to that effect[29] (even though the Covenant itself states that it can only be amended by an extraordinary PNC session).[30] In the event, rather than amend the Covenant, the PNC demonstratively reaffirmed its authority in the Preamble of the Political Declaration (see Appendix 1). Apparently the PLO's position was that the validity of the unamended Covenant had to be preserved until after a Palestinian state had been set up. A document published by a Lebanese daily and said to be the PLO's settlement plan (see above) indeed implied that the PLO's attitude to the Covenant might change after the Palestinians' "elementary rights" had been granted and a Palestinian state established.[31]

A series of 12 meetings on the Palestinian question was held in France in the second half of 1976 and the first quarter of 1977 between PLO members and representatives of the Israel Council for Israeli-Palestinian Peace, through the mediation of French Jewish and Left-wing figures. The PLO team at the meetings—which, according to press reports, were initiated by the PLO—was headed by 'Isām Sartāwī, and consisted only of Fatḥ members. Sartāwī's Israeli counterpart was Professor Mattityahu Peled (a General in the reserves).

The very fact that the meetings were being held produced heated debate within the PLO. Criticism was voiced by pro-Syrian personalities such as Zuhayr Muḥsin, by Fatḥ leaders like Fārūq Qaddūmī, and by Rejectionist spokesmen, all contending that the meetings were not authorized by competent PLO bodies, and were in violation of the principles of the Palestinian National Covenant. The pro-Syrians further criticized the Fath members who conducted the meetings for having taken such an important step without co-ordination with the Arab governments. The PDFLP's denunciation of the meeting was based on the argument that the Israel Council for Israeli-Palestinian Peace was a pro-Zionist group.

Members of the PLO team at the meetings insisted that they had been authorized by Yāsir 'Arafāt. But the head of the PLO Political Department, Fārūq Qaddūmī (a member of the PLO Executive Committee) denied that the EC had authorized the meetings. According to him, they were "a result of individual initiative and have absolutely nothing to do with the PLO or its representatives."[32] It appears likely that if 'Arafāt did indeed give his consent to the meetings, he did so in a personal, non-official capacity.

The main outcome of the meetings was a joint statement issued in Paris on 1 January 1977 and signed by Peled and, according to him, by a PLO representative (probably Sartāwī). In the published statement, the PLO affirmed that its policy was one of "striving for a peaceful solution of the Israeli-Palestinian conflict on the basis of the mutual acceptance of the principles of freedom, sovereignty and security for both peoples."[33] Furthermore, the PLO considered the principles of the manifesto of the Israel Council for Israeli-Palestinian Peace "as an adequate basis for solving the Israeli-Palestinian conflict."[34] (The Council's manifesto of February 1976 upheld the Zionist character of Israel and supported her pre-1967 boundaries.)

Again, as in the case of Sartāwī's letter to Kreisky, the PLO's Political Department denied that any responsible or authorized member of the PLO had signed the Paris statement. Fārūq Qaddūmī stated that the PLO had not permitted any of its members to take part in the meetings, and that reports of a PLO representative having signed an agreement with Peled were groundless.[35] In March, the opponents of the meetings had the upper hand in the PNC's deliberations on the issue. The PNC affirmed the significance of establishing relations and co-ordinating with those "progressive and democratic Jewish forces inside and outside the occupied Homeland" that are struggling against Zionism as a doctrine and in practice."[36] Similarly, the PNC plenary approved the recommendation of its Committee for Affairs of the Occupied Homeland, that "the PNC affirm the importance of supporting progressive and democratic forces that are *hostile to Zionism*."[37] Following the PNC session, the Israeli team discontinued the meetings presumably because, in the light of the PNC resolutions, their continuation would have been interpreted in Israel as readiness on its part to be characterized as anti-Zionist.

An evaluation of the PLO's motives in undertaking these meetings is made difficult by the contradictory attitudes towards them within the PLO itself. It is not unlikely that some PLO personalities sought a channel of communication with leading Israeli figures, and believed that those attending the meetings (who included persons with notable records in the army, in government or in party politics) would be able to provide it. It is also likely that the PLO sought to exploit the meetings to gain legitimacy in the eyes of American Jewry, and to facilitate a dialogue between leading American Jews and its own representatives. The contacts Peled and Sartāwī had with members of the American Jewish community in the US in November and December 1976 would indicate such an intention. At the same time, the meetings may have been intended by the PLO to weaken the Israeli government's position (at home and abroad) rejecting recognition of, and a dialogue with, the PLO. A document published in a Kuwaiti paper and described as a "secret Fath circular", stated that the meetings were indeed held in order "to deepen internal contradictions" in Israel, with the effect of "destroying the Zionist existence from within."[38]

The view that the meetings formed part of the PLO's political warfare against Israel gained validity from reports that the team which supervised the Paris meetings was also in charge of the PLO's counter-immigration campaign to encourage emigration of oriental Jews from Israel back to their Arab countries of origin. This campaign was led by Maḥmūd 'Abbās (code-named Abū Māzin), a member of al-Fatḥ's Central Committee, who specialized in evaluating internal weaknesses of the "Israeli-Zionist society" and in devising ways to increase them.[39] He had worked to persuade Arab governments to offer restoration of citizenship to former Jewish nationals who had emigrated to Israel and were now willing to return. The PNC's Committee for Affairs of the Occupied Homeland had appealed to all Arab governments to co-operate in this scheme.[40] Between 1975 and 1977, most Arab states accepted the arrangement—Jordan, Libya and Lebanon being the exceptions. Saudi Arabia was said to have undertaken to cover the necessary expenses involved.

By mid-1977, however, the quantitative achievement of the campaign was limited: Morocco was the only country to attract more than a few individuals. According to the PLO's own figures of February 1977, no more than 4,500 families (i.e. presumably some 20,000 persons) emigrated there from Israel.[41] Other Arab press accounts published later set that figure at no more than 1,000 persons.[42]

The campaign drew criticism from Palestinian and other Arab commentators. They argued that if large numbers of oriental Jews left Israel, the severity of the internal contradictions between oriental and occidental Jews would diminish; that mass immigration of additional occidental Jews would become possible; that the Jews returning to Arab countries would form a "fifth column [of] agents and spies ready to work for Israel"; that they would exploit the economies of their Arab host countries and "drink their oil"; and finally, that since the Jews were "evil by nature", they would corrupt the countries to which they returned.[43]

Following the PNC's decision to promote contacts with anti-Zionist forces in Israel, the PLO intensified its communications with the Communist Party (Rakah). Members of the PLO and of Rakah had had occasional informal talks in the past, but the first official and public joint meeting took place in Prague on 3-4 May 1977. The PLO delegation was headed by Mājid Abū Sharāra, member of al-Fatḥ's Revolutionary Council; and the Rakah delegation by Emil Tu'ma, member of its Political Bureau.

The Prague meeting drew fire from several directions. Iraq and pro-Iraqi Palestinian groups argued that Rakah was a Zionist party, which formed part of the "racial expansionist Zionist entity's structure."[44] Pro-Syrian elements in the PLO (in keeping with their negation of independent Palestinian action) criticized the meeting because it had not been sanctioned by the major Arab governments.

Supporters of the meeting (Maḥmūd 'Abbās, Nā'if Ḥawātima and others) defended Rakah as an anti-Zionist party, and maintained that the meeting was approved by the PLO's EC. Along with other Arab observers, they also claimed that it would likely help Rakah in its campaign to win over Arab voters from the Israel Council for Israeli-Palestinian Peace in the imminent Israeli elections.[45] According to the PDFLP's weekly, helping Rakah's election campaign in this way was one of the purposes of the Prague meeting.[46]

The establishment of formal PLO-Rakah contacts should also be seen against the background in 1976 and 1977 of a fundamental change in the PLO's view of Israeli Arabs and their role in the Palestinian struggle against Israel. In the past, the dominant PLO view had been that Arab citizens of Israel could not be relied upon in that struggle, and that efforts should concentrate on enlisting public opinion as well as recruiting individual activists in the territories occupied in June 1967.

The rise of Palestinian nationalism among Israeli Arabs—dramatically demonstrated by the events of the "Day of the Land" (30 March 1976)—gradually changed that view. The new trend was reflected in the recommendations adopted by the PNC in March 1977, which offered guidelines for a campaign designed to involve Israeli Arab citizens in the struggle against Israel. These guidelines referred to PLO support for Israeli Arabs in economic, educational and cultural affairs; envisaged PLO help in preventing the emigration of Arabs from Israel and the sale of Arab land to Jews; provided for a more significant share in the manning of PLO bodies to be granted to Israeli Arabs; and called for greater PLO attention to Israeli Arab affairs.[47]

THE PLO'S RELATIONS WITH ARAB GOVERNMENTS

RELATIONS WITH SYRIA

The end of the Lebanese civil war in October 1976 saved the PLO from military collapse and enabled it to maintain some political freedom of action, even under the conditions of Syrian occupation. Al-Fatḥ's military organization was damaged but not broken, and the PLO retained its hold over the internal affairs of the refugee camps. Yet the end of the war did not put an end to Syria's efforts to bring the PLO under her control. In resisting those efforts, the PLO found succour with Saudi Arabia and, to a lesser extent, with Egypt and Kuwait (the members, alongside Syria, of the quadripartite ceasefire committee established in Lebanon under the Riyadh resolutions).

Eventually, a PLO-Syrian understanding on a *modus vivendi* in Lebanon began to emerge, and was formalized in the Shtūrā Agreement of 25 July 1977 (see below). It resulted from the gradually developing convergence of their points of view on issues related to the Geneva conference and to developments in southern Lebanon—a convergence which, in the summer of 1977, brought the two sides closer together than they had been since the Syrians first turned against the PLO early in 1976.

In the interval, however, PLO-Syrian relations were dominated by tensions created by President Asad's concept of the Palestinian issue in general, and of the role of the PLO in particular. That concept rejected separate Palestinian nationalism and nationhood: the Palestinians should form part of a larger political unit embracing Syria, Lebanon and Jordan as well as Palestine. The struggle for Palestinian territory was thus not viewed by Syria as the exclusive concern of the

Palestinians or specifically of the PLO. The latter should therefore not act independently in the conflict against Israel or over other issues, but should coordinate its steps with its Arab allies—first and foremost with Syria.

Syrian pressures on the PLO operated along three lines: to obtain PLO acceptance of a Lebanese solution on Syria's terms; to push through organizational changes in the PLO to increase Syrian influence in it (see above); and to induce the PLO to consent to a dialogue with Jordan.

In Lebanon, Syrian objectives were:

1. Restriction of Palestinian autonomy, which had been based on the PLO's military control of the refugee camps and adjacent areas. For this purpose, the number of armed Palestinians in the camps was to be limited; heavy arms were to be "collected" from the camps; the Arab Deterrent Force (ADF) and later the reconstituted Lebanese armed forces were to be given the right to enter the camps at their discretion.
2. Formation of a Syrian-controlled PLO military presence in southern Lebanon, absorbing Palestinian units and heavy arms formerly at large in the Lebanese cities.
3. Elimination of the pro-Iraqi elements of the Palestinian Rejection Front either by pro-Syrian Palestinian or Syrian forces.

Syria tried to achieve the first two objectives by pressuring the PLO into implementing the 1969 Cairo Agreement and its appendices which, according to her interpretation, regulate the Palestinian presence in Lebanon. (For the various interpretations of the Agreement, see chapter on Lebanon.)

Prior to Syria's intervention in Lebanon, the PLO felt that the 1969 Agreement had become irrelevant. Since its signature, the PLO had grown numerically and increased its military strength; its stature had been enhanced by being recognized by the Arab states as the sole representative of the Palestinians; the authority of the Lebanese government had become shaky; and the PLO had effectively allied itself with local political movements in Lebanon. The PLO thus felt justified in claiming exclusive authority over the refugee camps and over Palestinian activities elsewhere in Lebanon. It insisted that Palestinians must have the right to carry on their struggle against Israel unhindered, with freedom to move and carry arms anywhere in the country, as well as to maintain a military presence and store heavy weapons at any point of their choosing in southern Lebanon.

Under Syrian pressures from January 1976, PLO leaders declared their acceptance of the Cairo Agreement as the basis of a Lebanese settlement but dragged their feet whenever the question of its implementation came up. Following the Syrian offensive of September and October 1976, the Cairo Agreement became—ironically enough—an asset to the PLO. In the face of Syrian pressures and the Maronite attempts to rid Lebanon of the Palestinians altogether, the Cairo Agreement—expressly reaffirmed by the Riyadh and Cairo conferences of October 1976—symbolized the all-Arab legitimization of the Palestinian presence in Lebanon. When Christian-Lebanese spokesmen declared in May 1977 that the Cairo Agreement was null and void because the Palestinians had refused to implement it, and that their presence in Lebanon had therefore become illegal, the PLO asserted emphatically and repeatedly that, according to its own interpretation, it had in fact implemented most clauses of the Agreement. But this clearly contradicted Syria's understanding of the Agreement, according to which PLO military movements outside the refugee camps would have been restricted; its heavy arms handed over to the Syrian-dominated ADF, and its armed presence in the camps sharply reduced. ADF units would also have been entitled to enter the refugee camps.

These disagreements came to a head in February 1977 when Syria brought stronger pressures to bear on the PLO. These included closure of PLO bases and training camps, and harassment of PLO members in Syria; Syrian military concentrations around Beirut refugee camps, accompanied by threats to break into the camps; and closure of the "clandestine" PLO radio station in Lebanon (Voice of Palestine). Syrian military measures in Beirut were rescinded apparently as a result of Saudi intervention, and following a conciliatory message from 'Arafāt to Asad on 15 February 1977. Saudi Arabia, in co-operation with Egypt and Kuwait, rescued the PLO from the application of the Syrian interpretation by creating a majority against it in the quadripartite ceasefire committee. Accordingly, in March 1977, the committee refused to endorse the Syrian interpretation.[48]

Meanwhile, a PLO-Syrian understanding on Lebanon was beginning to evolve against the background of developments in the south, which both considered unfavourable. The transfer of Palestinian forces from northern and central Lebanon to the south (especially to the "Fatahland" area) in late 1976 and early 1977, and the emergence of the Maronite-Israeli alliance (see survey of Lebanon), led to hostilities between the PLO and their Lebanese allies on the one hand, and the forces of the Christian enclaves on the other, with each side trying to enlarge the territory under its control. A successful Christian offensive in March 1977 widened the area accessible from Israel by means of the "Good Fence", and threatened to close the territorial gap separating two of its three enclaves, thereby cutting off some of the besieging PLO forces.

Early in April, the PLO launched a major counter-offensive designed to regain ground lost in March. Syria—likewise opposed to the Christian advance and interested in the transfer of further PLO forces to the south—permitted the passage of large Palestinian reinforcements into the south through Syrian-held areas. Furthermore, Syria supported the counter-offensive through the participation of al-Sā'iqa units, and by letting the PLO use heavy artillery emplacements in the Syrian-held area. The PLO regained the ground it had lost in March, as well as an important town (al-Khiyām) surrendered in February. Syria did not encourage further PLO advances, on the assumption that they would provoke Israeli counter-action. Instead it sought to persuade the PLO that the termination of the Israeli-Maronite alliance and the closure of the "Good Fence" would be made easier by implementing the Cairo Agreement throughout Lebanon. This would lead to the re-establishment of the Lebanese government's authority in the south.

The accelerated preparations for reconvening the Geneva conference also augmented the PLO's interest in reaching an accord with Syria. By ending the dispute with Syria in Lebanon, PLO leaders expected to enhance their prospects of making a mark in the ME conflict. A PLO-Syrian understanding on implementing the Cairo Agreement was now worked out, and formalized on 25 July 1977 in the PLO-Syrian-Lebanese agreement of Shtūrā (for its main provisions, see chapter on Lebanon).

Under the agreement (whose text was kept secret, but which was partially reported in the Lebanese press), the PLO recognized the sovereignty of the Lebanese government over Lebanese territory and its inhabitants in a way which could imply the restoration of Lebanese sovereignty over the refugee camps. The PLO also accepted the principle that only Palestinians who had already been domiciled in Lebanon when the Cairo Agreement was signed in 1969 had a right to reside there now. These two aspects of the Shtūrā agreement—if translated into practice—constituted a setback for the PLO.

On the other hand, the agreement entrusted security within the refugee camps to the PLO's military police force; did not place numerical limits on the number of PLO supporters allowed to carry light arms in the camps, or on the quantities of light arms held there (which had been a controversial issue); and laid down that Lebanese army troops would only enter the camps in co-ordination with the PLO military command. The agreement did not prohibit PLO operations against Israel from southern Lebanon, though it called for the withdrawal of all (or almost all) PLO units to a distance of 15 kms from the Israeli border in the western and central sectors of south Lebanon, and for their concentration in the eastern sector, the 'Arqūb area ("Fatḥland").[49]

A full evaluation of the PLO's gains and losses in Lebanon following the Shtūrā Agreement can only be attempted after its details are fully disclosed and the extent of its implementation becomes known.

In the period between the Riyadh and Cairo conferences and the 13th PNC session (i.e. October 1976 till March 1977), PLO opposition to Syria's line in Lebanon caused the latter to try and bring about changes within the PLO in her favour. In particular, Syria brought pressure to bear for the enlargement of the PNC (hitherto numbering 187 members) by as many as 200 pro-Syrian and pro-Jordanian delegates, who would not belong to any of the PLO's constituent fidā'ī organizations (see above). This step was meant to end, or at least to weaken, al-Fatḥ's dominant position in the PNC. There was even a call by the Syrian government daily for the new PNC to exclude fidā'ī representatives altogether.[50]

The Syrian government also threatened to set up an alternative Palestinian leadership more co-operative towards itself.[51] Addressing the PLO CC convening in Damascus, President Asad presumably wished to convey the desirability of a change in the PLO leadership when he pointed to the importance of the CC's "making a wider and more comprehensive assessment and analysis of what has taken place on the Lebanese scene, in order to draw the conclusions needed and to absorb them in a way which will *ensure that the Palestinian revolution does not slip into any mistakes*."[52] Zuhayr Muḥsin, head of al-Sā'iqa (as usual putting the Syrian line more forcefully than official Syrian spokesmen), explicitly called for the removal of the existing PLO leadership.[53] To back her demands, Syria applied military pressure against the PLO in Beirut in February 1977, and took steps against PLO installations and personnel in Syria, as mentioned above.

Syria listed the major decisions which it expected the PNC's March 1977 session to take. These included acceptance of a Palestinian state on any "liberated" part of Palestine; normalization of PLO-Jordanian relations; the formation of a "strategic PLO-Syrian front"[54] (implying close political co-ordination between the two); re-examination of the Palestinian National Covenant and the PLO's Fundamental Statute (*al-niẓām al-asāsī*); and the exercise of self-criticism (presumably leading to changes in leadership).[55] Syria underlined these expectations by allowing the party organ to quote from an internal party publication, *al-Munādil*, the contents of which were not usually made public.

Although the PNC was enlarged, al-Fatḥ succeeded in maintaining its dominant position, and Syria's expectations were expressly met only with regard to the first of the above points. Yet it would be correct to say that, by avoiding any reference in its resolutions and statements to Syria's role in Lebanon and to Jordan's record *vis-à-vis* the PLO, the PNC was in fact displaying some accommodation towards Syria. Had any official reference been made, it could in the circumstances only have been hostile. Even so, one-third of the delegates did not vote for the pro-Syrian PNC chairman candidate, Khālid al-Fāhūm (172 delegates voted for him, 69 against, 21 abstained, and 27 were absent).

RELATIONS WITH SAUDI ARABIA

Lacking an independent territorial base and substantial military and financial resources of its own, the PLO has traditionally sought to use inter-Arab discords to keep its freedom of action from being encroached upon by any single Arab government. Syria's drive to consolidate its influence over the PLO led the latter to seek a counterweight by improving relations with Saudi Arabia. Other considerations on the part of the PLO included Saudi influence in the US, and the fact that Riyadh was its largest single financial backer.

Saudi Arabia's interests were to prevent the PLO from becoming a Syrian satellite; to keep it from drawing too close to the Soviet Union; to foster al-Fath so as to neutralize radical elements within the PLO liable to foment revolutionary agitation in the ME in general, and in Saudi Arabia in particular; and to draw the PLO into the political process and into a dialogue with the US.

As a result, PLO-Saudi ties improved considerably during the period under review, despite substantial ideological opposition within the PLO. The visit by a Fatḥ delegation to Saudi Arabia in January 1977 was a major step in that development. The leading figure in the delegation was Salāḥ Khalaf (code-named Abū Ayyād), who had been in command of military operations during the Lebanese war. Relative to the overall ideological stance of al-Fatḥ, he was widely considered to represent the "leftist" or radical trend. His participation in the delegation constituted a significant PLO gesture towards Saudi Arabia—a country usually associated in Palestinian ideology with "imperialism and reaction."

Saudi Arabia apparently urged the PLO to demonstrate moderation in the PNC session, and to adopt positive resolutions on PLO relations with Jordan and on the formation of a government-in-exile. It also helped the PLO to withstand Syrian pressure in Lebanon in March 1977 by refusing (along with Egypt and Kuwait) to approve the Syrian-backed interpretation of the Cairo Agreement. Saudi Arabia supported PLO efforts to enhance its political standing in the West Bank through financial aid to West Bank municipalities. Saudi Arabia was also instrumental in the indirect PLO-US contacts held during the period under review, aimed at bringing about American recognition of the PLO.

RELATIONS WITH EGYPT

Like Saudi Arabia, Egypt shared the PLO's interest in blocking Syria's attempts to bring the organization under her control. Following the crisis produced by the conclusion of the second Sinai disengagement agreement of September 1975, PLO-Egyptian relations improved in 1976, mirroring the deterioration of PLO-Syrian relations in Lebanon. As early as January 1976, Egypt demonstrated her support of the PLO's stand in Lebanon by dispatching Palestinian units stationed in Egypt to fight alongside the PLO.[56]

Egypt initiated a move to admit Palestine, represented by the PLO, as a full member of the Arab League in September 1976. (Hitherto, the PLO had the status of "non-voting member.") The Egyptian step was intended, *inter alia*, to consolidate Yāsir 'Arafāt's leadership in the face of Syrian military and political pressures. President Sādāt said at the time that the preservation of 'Arafāt's leadership was a principle of Egyptian policy.[57] In Lebanon, Egypt joined Saudi Arabia and Kuwait in preventing the approval of the Syrian-backed interpretation of the Cairo Agreement (see above). On 18 June 1977, following closer PLO-Egyptian contacts, a Joint Co-ordination Committee was formed (a similar committee being established simultaneously between the PLO and Syria). Nonetheless, this Egyptian support did not eliminate PLO suspicions concerning Cairo's willingness to stand by its public commitments to the PLO; neither did it resolve disagreements on central issues related to the ME conflict.

One such issue was the PLO-Jordanian link. In order to facilitate a rapid reconvening of the Geneva conference and to encourage a US-PLO dialogue, Egypt proposed the establishment of formal PLO-Jordanian ties prior to the conference and, in January 1977, advocated a formal link between Jordan and any future Palestinian state. The PLO regarded the Egyptian proposal as contradicting Egypt's public endorsement of the principle of Palestinian independence. Egypt hinted that the idea was merely an expedient and did not necessarily reflect its genuine attitude on the Palestinian issue. Vice-President Mubārak, for example, was quoted as stating that President Sādāt's intention was to prevent Israel from blocking the Geneva conference on the pretext of opposition to a Palestinian state.[58] Nevertheless, the PLO reacted coolly to the idea. Its spokesmen insisted that only the Palestinian people themselves could decide on their future relations with any Arab state, and would do so only after their sovereignty was finally established.[59]

Another measure Egypt urged on the PLO was to form a Palestinian government-in-exile, an idea she had advocated since 1972. Egypt argued that the creation of such a government would lead to wider international recognition of the PLO; would weaken Israel's argument against its recognition; and would pave the way for the establishment of a Palestinian state.[60] The Egyptian initiative over full PLO membership in the Arab League was presumably connected with this idea. At the time of writing, however, the PLO had neither agreed to formal ties with Jordan prior to the Geneva conference, nor had it formed a government-in-exile.

Another area of disagreement was over the Palestinian National Covenant: Sādāt had reportedly assured the US Secretary of State that the PNC would amend the Covenant; but when the PNC convened, it did nothing of the kind.

RELATIONS WITH JORDAN

Under Syrian pressure—and with Saudi and Egyptian encouragement—the CC meeting on 23 January 1977 instructed the EC to open a dialogue with Jordan. This was followed by a PLO-Jordanian working meeting (22-25 February 1977) in Amman, and by talks between 'Arafāt and King Ḥusayn in Cairo (8 March 1977).

The dialogue met with fierce opposition from Rejectionist organizations and from Nā'if Ḥawātima's PDFLP. On the other hand, pro-Syrian personalities in the PLO tried to justify the talks. Zuhayr Muḥsin, for instance, re-emphasized Jordan's role in the conflict with Israel: "Jordan is a confrontation state in addition to her special and historical responsibility to the West Bank and the Palestinian problem." He thus gave support to Jordan's claim for an active role in resolving the Palestinian question, exceeding the one assigned to her by the 1974 Rabat resolutions. Muḥsin went so far as to say that the PLO leadership rather than Jordan had been responsible for the armed conflict in 1970 and 1971[61]—a statement tantamount to heresy when compared with the accepted PLO version of those events. Another way of justifying the dialogue was that it would put the PLO in a better position to play a more direct role in West Bank affairs.[62]

In actual fact, however, the PLO-Jordan meetings did nothing whatsoever to reduce the fundamental conflict of interests between them—being locked in what both considered as a struggle for survival. In King Ḥusayn's view, Jordan was itself a Palestinian state: an independent state in the West Bank was certain to bring an end to his dynasty by drawing the political loyalty of the Palestinian majority in Jordan away from the Hashemites. The PLO, on the other hand, insisted on a completely independent Palestinian state. Furthermore, Article Two of the Palestinian National Covenant was worded in such a way that "Palestine" could be meant to include the East Bank. Many Palestinian nationalists considered the overthrow of the Hashemite monarchy as a primary Palestinian goal.

In the period under discussion, Jordan worked systematically to reassert her claim and her position on the West Bank (see chapter on Jordan). The PLO, for its part, endeavoured to contain Jordan's influence. It tried, for example, to make West Bank municipalities less dependent on Jordan by providing financial aid from other Arab states. Since funds contributed by Saudi Arabia and the Gulf Emirates had to be transferred through Jordan, however, they could not reach the municipalities without Jordanian consent.

Jordan's opening position in the dialogue was to favour the concept of a federation of both banks, as originally outlined in 1972 in King Ḥusayn's "United Arab Kingdom Plan."[63] The PLO's opening position, as laid down in the resolution approving the dialogue, was that PLO-Jordanian relations must be based on the Rabat resolutions. Under their terms, the PLO argued, Jordan was obliged to facilitate the resumption of the PLO's political and military presence in Jordan; to co-operate with the PLO in extending economic support to the population of the occupied territories; and to permit fidā'ī activity against Israel across her borders. Typical of the PLO's rejection of Jordan's renewed "United Arab Kingdom Plan" was Fārūq Qaddūmi's assertion that "there must be an independent Palestinian state with an independent parliament and independent government, as well as its own independent army and independent diplomatic representation."[64]

The meetings resulted in some minor gestures, such as the release of several PLO members from Jordanian jails (February 1977). Reports of Jordanian consent to the resumption of fidā'ī presence in Jordan were denied by PLO leaders;[65] nor were they borne out by subsequent developments. In all substantive respects, the meetings left the situation exactly as it had been before.

RELATIONS WITH IRAQ AND LIBYA

The Syrian-Egyptian *rapprochement* set into motion at the Riyadh conference in October 1976 weakened the relative positions of Iraq and Libya, and consequently their impact on PLO affairs. Both countries continued to offer financial and military support to Palestinian organizations, particularly to those belonging to the Rejection Front. Yet on the whole the ability of those two "rejection" states to influence the PLO had decreased.

Unable to employ her own regular military units in Lebanon after the Riyadh and Cairo conferences, Iraq continued her campaign against Syria there by proxy—mainly by means of the pro-Iraqi faction headed by Abū al-'Abbās (see above). Throughout the first half of 1977, this group was engaged in violent skirmishes with pro-Syrian groups, such as Aḥmad Jibrīl's faction and al-Sā'iqa. The PLO leadership, anxious to preserve some measure of unity after the Lebanese civil war, made repeated efforts to bring about a Syrian-Iraqi reconciliation, hoping thereby to end the inter-factional strife within its own ranks as well.

'Arafāt also engaged in mediating in the Egyptian-Libyan dispute. On the other hand, statements made during visits to Libya by the pro-Syrian rejectionist, Aḥmad Jibrīl, seemed to suggest some Palestinian involvement in a renewed Libyan-Syrian *rapprochement*.[66]

THE PLO AND THE USSR

The termination of the PLO-Syrian military confrontation in Lebanon helped to improve PLO-Soviet relations, which had been strained by what the PLO considered as an ambivalent Soviet position on the Syrian-PLO conflict, and by Soviet reluctance to back the PLO all the way. Al-Fatḥ's Salāḥ Khalaf—who ran the

PLO's military operation in Lebanon during the war—supposedly alleged that it was Moscow which gave the order to Syria to intervene militarily against the Palestinian resistance in Lebanon.[67]

After the war, the PLO sought increased Soviet military aid to re-equip its units. It also tried to enlist Soviet help to secure for the PLO the status of an independent and equal party to the ME settlement by exerting pressure on the US and, through her, on Israel. Marxist and other anti-Saudi elements in the PLO were also interested in closer relations with the USSR as a counterweight to Saudi influence on the organization.

However there were also conflicts of interests between the PLO and the USSR on several issues. The most important of these were Soviet recognition of Israel's right to exist; Soviet support of Resolution 242; the PLO's relations with Saudi Arabia; and Jewish emigration from the USSR to Israel. Another major issue of disagreement was the manner and timing of PLO participation at Geneva. While supporting independent PLO participation and firmly rejecting the idea of a PLO-Jordanian tie, the USSR was understood in late 1976 to have considered postponing full PLO participation until the second stage of the Geneva conference. Thus at first, the PLO would only participate in the work of sub-committees. The Soviet concept was intended to circumvent the procedural difficulties likely to be raised by Israel. Another Soviet proposal was to reconvene the peace conference without the PLO, but to place the question of PLO participation on the agenda at its first session.

A speech by Brezhnev on 21 March 1977, in which he outlined a ME settlement plan without mentioning the PLO by name, was closely followed by the visit of a high-level PLO delegation to Moscow (4–8 April 1977). The composition of the delegation—which included leading members of al-Fatḥ, al-Sāʿiqa, the PDFLP, ALF, and PFLP-GC (Jibrīl's faction)—reflected PLO concern over Soviet positions. The marked publicity given to the visit by the Soviet side reflected Moscow's interest in promoting Soviet-PLO relations to a significantly higher level of political co-operation. The visit was highlighted by the first official meeting ever of ʿArafāt with Brezhnev. Moscow stated its commitment to Palestinian people's rights, including the right to establish an "independent Palestinian state" (earlier Soviet references having been only to a "Palestinian state"). Despite the evident desire to play up the importance of the visit, the USSR did not commit itself to supporting PLO participation at Geneva from the start and on an equal footing with the other parties.

The PLO evinced anxiety over intimations of Moscow's intentions to resume diplomatic relations with Israel before the end of 1977 (the declared Soviet position being that a resumption of diplomatic relations was conditional upon Israeli withdrawal to pre-1967 lines). There was also concern over Soviet advocacy of PLO recognition of Israel. Nevertheless, advocates of PLO-Soviet co-operation continued to maintain that the PLO should make efforts to co-ordinate its position with the USSR. Some believed that the USSR was in actual fact committed to the right of the PLO to participate in Geneva on equal footing from the start.[68]

THE PLO AND THE US

The most important development in PLO-US relations in the period under review was the emergence of the Carter Administration's position on the Palestinian problem and the components it identified in a ME settlement. These included a "Homeland" for the Palestinians and a role for the PLO (see essay on "The US and the Middle East").

Until the advent of the Carter Administration, the PLO had usually considered itself to be struggling against the US and its Middle Eastern interests and allies, both in Lebanon and in Israel. Consequently, open animosity and deep mistrust had characterized PLO attitudes to Washington. After January 1977, official US statements met with mixed reactions in the PLO. Whereas Yāsir 'Arafāt stated on several occasions that the US position on the Palestinian issue had changed for the better, other leaders of al-Fatḥ, as well as of the other PLO member organizations, belittled its significance. The latter argued that even if some change had occurred, it could not bridge the fundamental and conflicting interests of the PLO and the US. "In spite of the American recognition of our rights", said Fārūq Qaddūmī, "which in itself is a step forward, we will never change our principled, permanent anti-imperialist position." He added:

> The US has participated on all levels in the creation and sustenance of Israel. Israel is an American strategic need, for the purpose of impeding the Arab liberation movement and of draining off the Arab nation's resources, through wars and conflicts and permanent pre-occupation [with Israel], thus retarding [Arab] economic advancement.[69]

This perception of US policies was doubtlessly influenced by the US making its recognition of the PLO conditional on the latter's recognition of Israel, and on the acceptance of Security Council Resolutions 242 and 338.

Official and unequivocal American recognition of the PLO was indeed a major goal of its leaders. But even before achieving that, direct contact with the US was seen as advantageous to the PLO: for one thing, it would be detrimental to Israel's international standing; for another, the PLO would no longer have to rely on any Arab state as go-between in transmitting its views to the US. Thus, while on the whole maintaining an anti-American posture, the PLO began actively to seek official American recognition late in 1976. To promote this objective, the PLO pursued several courses simultaneously. It attempted to obtain official status for PLO delegations and representatives in the US, and to maintain unofficial contacts with US officials, intended to lead eventually to full recognition. It also sought to improve the PLO's standing in US public opinion, and to project an image of moderation in the Western media generally. Finally, through its meetings with American Jewish leaders, the PLO sought to discredit the US position of non-recognition. In pursuing these tactics, Sabri Jiryīs and 'Isam Sartāwī, two PLO officers, registered their intention to open an information office in Washington with the US Department of Justice on 18 November 1976. They were turned down on the basis of incorrect information found in Jiryīs' visa application. Jiryīs was ordered to leave the US, but tried to return as soon as the Carter Administration took office. However, his visa application was again turned down—this time by Secretary Vance personally on 8 February 1977. Following the initial Jiryīs-Sartāwī setback, Qaddūmī stated that he knew neither who the two men were, nor the purpose of their mission.[70] Most probably, these attempts were approved and encouraged by Yāsir 'Arafāt without consulting the EC[71] (as was apparently also the case with the meetings conducted in Paris by Sartāwī and other PLO officers with members of the Israel Council for Israeli-Palestinian Peace; see above).

The US was reported to have first initiated indirect communication with the PLO in 1975. Contacts became more frequent during the civil war in Lebanon, mainly in connection with the safety of American civilians and diplomats there. On wider ME issues, the US contacted the PLO mainly through Egyptian, Saudi or European intermediaries; but also through direct but informal means. For example, on 24 June 1977 in London, ex-Senator William Scranton met with Bāsil 'Aql, a leading PLO representative in the West. In addition, there was the Cairo meeting between a

PLO officer and three US senators on 11 November 1976; Carter's public greeting of the PLO's UN representative at a UN reception on 3 March 1977; and the meeting between a US congressional delegation and 'Arafāt in Cairo on 12 July 1977.

Nevertheless, throughout the period under review, the US kept its commitment not to recognize the PLO officially as long as it did not recognize Israel's right to exist. Right up to the eve of the PNC session in March 1977, the US had entertained hopes that the PLO would moderate its position on this point. President Carter's statement, in which he employed the term "Homeland" for the Palestinians, was issued while the PNC was in session, and was apparently intended to encourage such moderation. It was received with satisfaction by 'Arafāt, who expressed his personal confidence in President Carter (17 March 1977). However, the statement was criticized by others in the PLO for failing to mention exactly where that "Homeland" should be established.

As described above, the PNC explicitly rejected Resolutions 242 and 338. On 21 March 1977, the State Department declared that the PNC resolutions "did not contribute" to the solution of the ME problem. Up to July 1977, US-PLO relations remained deadlocked—with the PLO unwilling to meet the conditions set by Washington for its official recognition, and with the US unwilling to drop those conditions.

NOTES

1. *Al-Ra'y al-'Āmm*, Kuwait; 14 March 1977.
2. *Al-Siyāsa*, Kuwait; 26 April 1977.
3. Iraqi News Agency (INA), 21 March—British Broadcasting Corporation, Summary of World Broadcasts, the ME and Africa (BBC), 23 March 1977. INA, 1 April—BBC, 2 April 1977.
4. INA, 21 March—BBC, 23 March 1977.
5. *Monday Morning*, Beirut; 17 July 1977.
6. *Trouw*, Amsterdam; 31 March 1977.
7. INA, 7 October—BBC, 9 October 1976. *Al-Nahār*, Beirut; 9 October 1976.
8. *Al-Ba'th*, Damascus; 10 October 1976.
9. INA, 14 May—BBC, 16 May 1977.
10. Points 2 and 3 of the PNC's Political Declaration (see Appendix 1).
11. Point 15 of the Political Declaration (see Appendix 1).
12. Fārūq Qaddūmī (head of the PLO Political Department, and Secretary of al-Fatḥ's Central Committee), *Newsweek*, 7 March 1977.
13. Fārūq Qaddūmī, *Shu'ūn Filastīniyya*, 67 (June 1977), p. 40. Similarly: *al-Mustaqbal*, Paris; 2 July 1977. Nā'if Ḥawātima, *al-Ra'y al-'Āmm*, 19 March 1977.
14. *Al-Ahrām*, Cairo; 18 December 1976.
15. Point 11 of the Political Declaration (see Appendix 1).
16. R Cairo, Voice of Palestine, 21 March—Daily Report (DR), 22 March 1977.
17. Fārūq Qaddūmī in *al-Nahār*, 27 February 1977. R Cairo, Voice of Palestine, 11 May—DR, 11 May 1977. *Al-Mustaqbal*, 2 July 1977. Khālid Fāhūm, *al-Ra'y al-'Āmm*, 27 May 1977, p. 10.
18. Point 9 in the Political Declaration (see Appendix 1).
19. Mahmūd 'Abbās (alias Abū Māzin), *al-Anwār*, Beirut; 5 January 1977. 'Arafāt's interview with the *Washington Post*, 28 May 1977.
20. *Al-Nahār*, 31 July 1977.
21. *Al-Ahrām*, 26 February 1977. Qaddūmī in *Monday Morning*, Beirut; 2 May 1977. Also, *Shu'ūn Filastīniyya*, June 1977, p. 41.
22. *Al-Ahrām*, 8 and 10 December 1976.
23. *Al-Ahrām*, 26 November 1976. Qatar News Agency (*QNA*) 4 January—DR, 4 January 1977. *Al-Siyāsa*, 2 February 1977. *Akhir Sā'a*, Cairo; 2 March and 6 July 1977.
24. Voice of Palestine (Clandestine broadcast from Lebanon), 2 June—BBC, 4 June 1977.
25. See *Ākhir Sā'a*, 16 March 1977.
26. INA, 1 June—BBC, 3 June 1977. Also: Voice of Palestine (Clandestine) 30 December 1976—DR, 3 January 1977.

27. *Arbeiter-Zeitung*, Vienna; 13 February—DR, 14 February 1977.
28. *Al-Ahrām*, 26 February—DR, 1 March 1977.
29. See Nabil Sha'ath, *Washington Post*, 18 November 1977.
30. See Article 29 of the 1964 version of the Covenant, and Article 33 of the 1968 version.
31. *Al-Nahār*, 31 July 1977.
32. *Al-Ahrām*, 26 February 1977.
33. *Ha-Olam ha-Zeh*, Tel Aviv; 5 January 1977.
34. *Ibid.*
35. Saudi News Agency (*SNA*), 2 January—DR, 4 January 1977.
36. Point 14 of the 15-point Political Declaration (see Appendix 1).
37. Point 4 of the Committee's Recommendations, R Cairo, Voice of Palestine, 22 March—BBC, 25 March 1977.
38. Quoted in *al-Siyāsa*, 29 April—DR, 9 May 1977.
39. Maḥmūd 'Abbās expounded the theoretical basis of the counter-immigration campaign and the methods of its implementation in his book *Zionism, Beginning and End*, published by al-Fatḥ and prefaced by 'Arafāt (Abū Mazin, *al-sahyūniyya, bidāya wa-nihāya*, al-Fatḥ, Maktab al-Ta'bi'a wa-l-Tanzīm, 1 January 1976).
40. Point 5 of the Committee's Recommendations, R Cairo, Voice of Palestine, 22 March—BBC, 25 March 1977.
41. Qaddūmī in al-Ahrām, 26 February—DR, 1 March 1977.
42. *Al-Hawādith*, Beirut; 22 April 1977. *Al-Sayyād*, Beirut; 26 May 1977.
43. Dr As'ad 'Abd al-Rahmān, "The Return of the Jewish Arabs," *Shu'un Filastīniyya* (July, August, September 1976), pp. 99-109. Similar Palestinian and Syrian criticism in *al-Ba'th*, Damascus; 23 May 1977.
44. R Baghdad, 11 May—DR, 17 May 1977. INA, 12 May—DR, 12 May 1977.
45. *Al-Mustaqbal*, 28 May 1977.
46. *Al-Ḥurriyya*, Beirut; 16 May 1977.
47. Recommendations of the Committee for Affairs of the Occupied Homeland, approved by the PNC, R Cairo, Voice of Palestine, 22 March—BBC, 25 March 1977; and recommendations of the Cultural Committee approved by the PNC, R Cairo, Voice of Palestine, 28 March—BBC, 31 March 1977.
48. *Al-Sayyād*, 7 April 1977. *Al-Nahār*, 25 May 1977.
49. *Al-Usbū al-'Arabī*, Beirut; 25 July, 1 August 1977.
50. *Al-Ba'th*, 24 November 1976.
51. *Al-Hadaf*, Kuwait; 16 December 1976.
52. Syrian Arab News Agency (SANA), 14 December—DR, 14 December 1976. Emphasis added.
53. SANA, 28 January—DR, 28 January 1977.
54. *Al-Talā'ī* (organ of al-Sā'iqa), 15 March 1977.
55. Quoted in *al-Ba'th*, 1 February 1977.
56. The 1,000 troops of the 'Ayn Jālūt Brigade of the Palestine Liberation Army.
57. *Al-Ahrām*, 25 September 1976.
58. *Al-Mustaqbal*, 30 April 1977.
59. Khālid al-Ḥasan, quoted by Middle East News Agency (MENA), 2 January—DR, 3 January 1977. Maḥmud 'Abbās in *al-Anwār*, 5 January 1977.
60. Editorials in *al-Ahrām*, 10 October; 8, 10, 11 December 1976.
61. *Al-Ra'y*, Jordan; 31 January 1977. At the time the statement was made, Syria was pressing for changes in the PLO leadership.
62. Khālid al-Fahūm in *al-Akhabār*, Jordan; 23 February 1977. Also see *al-Thawra*, Damascus; 22 January 1977.
63. Statement by Jordanian Prime Minister in *al-Quds*, 23 June 1977.
64. *Al-Ahrām*, 26 February—DR, 1 March 1977.
65. Khālid al-Ḥasan quoted by QNA, 1 February—DR, 3 February 1977. Khālid al-Fāhūm in *al-Waṭan*, Kuwait; 21 April 1977.
66. R Tripoli, Voice of the Arab Homeland, 4 May—DR, 5 May 1977.
67. R Beirut, 26 September—DR, 27 September 1976.
68. See Zuhayr Muḥsin in *al-Usbū' al-'Arabī*, 9 May 1977.
69. *Shu'ūn Filastīniyya*, June 1977.
70. *Le Monde*, Paris; 21-22 November 1976.
71. MENA, 30 November 1976—DR, 1 December 1976.

Appendix 1: The PNC's Political Declaration and the Draft Political Programme presented to the PNC by the Rejection Front*

The 15-point Political Declaration adopted by the PNC, 20 March 1977 (MENA, 20 March 1977—BBC 22 March 1977).

Proceeding from the Palestine National Charter and the previous national council's resolutions; considering the decisions and political gains achieved by the PLO at the Arab and international levels during the period following the 12th session of the PNC; after studying and debating the latest developments in the Palestine issue; and stressing support for the Palestinian national struggle in the Arab and international forums, the PNC affirms the following:

1. The PNC affirms that the Palestine issue is the essence and the root of the Arab-Zionist conflict. Security Council Resolution 242 ignores the Palestinian people and their firm rights. The PNC therefore confirms its rejection of this resolution, and rejects negotiations at the Arab and international levels based on this Resolution.

2. The PNC affirms the stand of the PLO in its determination to continue the armed struggle, and its concomitant forms of political and mass struggle, to achieve our inalienable national rights.

3. The PNC affirms that the struggle, in all its military, political and popular forms, in the occupied territory constitutes the central link in its programme of struggle. On this basis, the PLO will strive to escalate the armed struggle in the occupied territory, to escalate all other concomitant forms of struggle and to give all kinds of moral support to the masses of our people in the occupied territory in

The 14-point draft Political Programme presented to the 13th PNC by the Front of Palestinian Forces Rejecting Capitulationist Settlements, 14 March 1977 (al-Thawrah Mustamirrah, Vol 1, No 9 [March 1977] pp. *8-9).*

1. The PNC affirms the PLO's position rejecting Security Council Resolution 242 and all the other resolutions leading to recognition of the Zionist entity and of its right to exist, and [the PNC also affirms] the PLO's refusal to interact on the basis of those resolutions in any Arab or international conference, including the Geneva conference.

3. The PNC affirms the PLO's complete adherence to the Palestinian National Covenant as the fundamental document guiding our struggle, and to the armed struggle as a fundamental strategy for that struggle, with all the concomitant forms of struggle.

6. The PNC affirms that the PLO regards the struggle in the occupied territory in all its military, political and popular forms as the central link in its [the PLO's] struggles and programmes. On this basis, the PLO strives to escalate the armed struggle in the occupied territory, to escalate all of its concomitant forms of struggle, and to give all kinds of material and moral support to our people in the

* The order of the clauses in the right-hand column has been rearranged so as to allow the reader to compare the stands of the two documents on the same issues. The number of the article as it originally appeared has been given.

order to escalate the struggle and to strengthen their steadfastness to defeat and liquidate the occupation.

4. The PNC affirms the PLO's stand which rejects all types of American capitulationist settlement and all liquidationist projects. The Council affirms the determination of the PLO to abort any settlement achieved at the expense of the firm national rights of our people. The PNC calls upon the Arab nation to shoulder its pan-Arab responsibilities and to pool all its energies to confront these imperialist and Zionist plans.

5. The PNC stresses the importance and necessity of national unity, both political and military, among all the contingents of the Palestine Revolution within the framework of the PLO, because this is one of the basic conditions for victory. For this reason, it is necessary to co-ordinate national unity at all levels and in all spheres on the basis of commitment to all these resolutions, and to draw up programmes which will ensure the implementation of this.

6. The PNC affirms the right of the Palestine Revolution to be present on the soil of fraternal Lebanon within the framework of the Cairo agreement and its appendices, concluded between the PLO and the Lebanese authorities. The Council also affirms adherence to the implementation of the Cairo agreement in letter and in spirit, including the preservation of the position of the Revolution and the security of the camps. The PNC refuses to accept any interpretation of this agreement by one side only. Meanwhile it affirms its eagerness for the maintenance of the sovereignty and security of Lebanon.

occupied land in order to reinforce and strengthen our people's steadfastness in the face of occupation.

2. The PNC affirms the PLO's rejection of the political settlement submitted at the present state of our people's struggle, the more so since the nature of that settlement has become clear: it is an imperialist, Zionist, reactionary settlement, and contradictory to our people's interests and to their inalienable historic rights. The PLO therefore struggles against that settlement and in order to thwart it.

4. The PNC affirms the PLO's awareness of the importance of national unity among all the contingents of the Palestinian Revolution, and of that unity being an essential condition to victory. The PLO therefore struggles for the consolidation of that unity on all levels, on the ground of the National Covenant and this programme, and of adherence thereto.

8. The PNC affirms the right of the Palestinian Revolution to be present on the soil of fraternal Lebanon, and its right to move and operate from it in the direction of the Zionist enemy in the occupied land. The PNC affirms the PLO's rejection of any one-sided interpretation to the Cairo agreement, and the PLO's adherence to all the achievements our masses scored in recent years on all levels.

7. The PNC greets the heroic fraternal Lebanese people and affirms the PLO's eagerness for the maintenance of the territorial integrity of Lebanon, the unity of its people and its security, independence, sovereignty and Arabism. The PNC affirms its pride in the support rendered by this heroic fraternal people to the PLO, which is struggling for our people to regain their national rights to their homeland and their right to return to this homeland. The PNC strongly affirms the need to deepen and consolidate cohesion between all Lebanese nationalist forces and the Palestine Revolution.

8. The PNC affirms the need to strengthen the Arab Front participating in the Palestine Revolution, and deepen cohesion with all forces participating in it in all Arab countries, as well as to escalate the joint Arab struggle and to further strengthen the Palestine Revolution in order to contend with the imperialist and Zionist designs.

9. The PNC has decided to consolidate Arab struggle and solidarity on the basis of struggle against imperialism and Zionism, to work for the liberation of all the occupied Arab areas, and to adhere to the support for the Palestine Revolution in order to regain the constant national rights of the Palestinian Arab people without any conciliation [*sulḥ*] or recognition [of Israel].

9. The PNC affirms the complete cohesion between the Palestinian Revolution and the masses of the Arab people in Lebanon and its nationalist and progressive forces. That cohesion was baptized in blood and in joint struggles in recent years. The PNC also affirms the Revolution's [active] effort to deepen and consolidate that cohesion and to put it in defined organizational, front-like[-*jabhawi*] frameworks.

11. The PNC affirms the complete cohesion of the Palestinian Revolution with the masses of the Arab people under the leadership of the Arab liberation movement in all Arab countries. These masses constitute the real strategic depth of the Revolution. The PLO struggles to advance the forms of struggle common to the different Arab national countries and to the contingents of the Arab liberation movements, and [the PLO struggles also] to arrive at a front-like [-*jabhawiyyah*] form, capable of leading the Arab people's masses in their struggles against all kinds of imperialist, Zionist, and reactionary presence in the Arab region.

5. The PNC affirms the PLO's firm position of refusing to recognize the Zionist entity, to make conciliation with it and to negotiate with it or with any of its limbs or extentions.

10. The PNC affirms the right of the PLO to exercise its struggle responsibilities at the pan-Arab level and through any Arab land, in the interest of liberating the occupied areas.	10. The PNC affirms the Palestinian Revolution's right and liberty to carry out armed struggle against the Zionist entity through any Arab land.
11. The PNC has decided to continue the struggle to regain the national rights of our people, in particular the right of return, self-determination and establishing an independent national state on their national soil.	No parallel clause in this document.
12. The PNC affirms the significance of co-operation and solidarity with socialist, non-aligned, Islamic and African countries, and with all the national liberation movements in the world.	12. The PNC affirms that the Palestinian Revolution led by the PLO is a part of the world front opposing imperialism, and of all the extensions, organs and detachments of that front. The PNC affirms the continuation of the Palestinian revolution's efforts to strengthen the alliance and joint struggle with the members of that front: the socialist states, the national liberation movements, and democratic and labour forces in capitalist countries.
13. The PNC hails the stands and struggles of all the democratic countries and forces against Zionism as one form of racism, as well as against its aggressive practices.	No parallel clause in this document.
14. The PNC affirms the significance of establishing relations and co-ordinating with the progressive and democratic Jewish forces inside and outside the occupied homeland, since these forces are struggling against Zionism as a doctrine and in practice. The PNC calls on all states and forces who love freedom, justice and peace in the world to end all forms of assistance to and co-operation with the racist Zionist regime, and to end contacts with it and its instruments.	14. The PNC affirms the significance of relations and co-ordination with progressive Jewish forces in the world which aim at the demolishing of the racist Zionist regime. The PNC denounces the contacts made with certain Zionists, and [denounces also] the memorandum presented to [Austria's chancellor] Kreisky.

15. Taking into consideration the important achievements in the Arab and international arenas since the conclusion of the PNC's 12th session, the PNC, which has reviewed the political report submitted by the PLO, has decided the following:
   a The Council confirms its wish for the PLO's rights to participate independently and on an equal footing in all the conferences and international forums concerned with the Palestine issue and the Arab-Zionist conflict, with a view to achieving our inalienable national rights as approved by the UN General Assembly in 1974, namely in Resolution 3236.
   b The Council declares that any settlement or agreement affecting the rights of our Palestinian people made in the absence of this people will be completely null and void.

No parallel clause in this document.

No parallel clause in this document.

7. The PNC affirms the PLO's position regarding the Jordanian regime, as this position is expressed in the resolutions of the PNC's past sessions.* [The PNC also affirms] the continuation of the PLO's struggle, through its cohesion with the masses of the Arab people of Jordan and its nationalist forces, for the establishment of a nationalist democratic order in Jordan.

No parallel clause in this document.

8. The PNC affirms the need to develop and advance the organizational form in the PLO, and to consolidate collective leadership, in order to reach a real front-like [-*jabhawi*] form [of organization].**

---

* This is a reference to the fifth point in the 12th PNC's 10-point Political Programme (adopted on 9 June 1974), stating that the PLO "will struggle together with the nationalist [namely: anti-Hashemite] Jordanian forces for the setting up of a national Jordanian-Palestinian front, with the goal of establishing a national democratic government in Jordan, which will unite with the Palestinian entity to be established [in Palestine] as the outcome of the struggle", and to earlier resolutions along that line adopted in each of the PNC sessions starting with the 8th session (28 February-5 March 1971).

** Essentially meaning equal power in PLO institutions (PNC, CC) to its member organizations regardless of their numerical strength.

Appendix 2
The PLO Executive Committee (as at 20 March 1977)

Yāsir ʻArafāt	al-Fatḥ	Chairman. C-in-C of the Palestine Revolution forces
Fārūq al-Qaddūmī	al-Fatḥ	Head of Political Dept
Zuhayr Muḥsin	al-Sāʻiqa	Head of Military Dept
ʻAbd al-Muḥsin Abu Maizar	Palestinian National Front —a West Bank group	Head of Pan-Arab and International Relations Dept Official spokesman of the EC; member of the Committee in charge of Dept of the Occupied Homeland*
Yāsir ʻAbd Rabbo	PDFLP	Head of Information and Culture Dept
ʻAbd al-Raḥīm Aḥmad	ALF	Head of Dept of Popular Organizations
Talāl Nājī	PFLP-GC, Jibrīl's faction	Head of Higher Education Dept
†Majdī Abu Ramadān	Independent, originally from Gaza. EC member for a short period in late 1967, early 1968	Head of Social Affairs Dept; Head of Central Bureau of Student Affairs, in Egypt
†Dr Aḥmad Sidqi al-Dajānī	Independent. Formerly member of Jordanian parliament. Member of EC for short period in 1968	Chairman of Higher Council of Education and Culture
Muḥammed Zuhdi al-Nashāshībi	al-Sāʻiqa	Head of Secretariat and Administrative Affairs
Wahīd Qamḥāwī	Palestinian National Front	Chairman of the Board of the Palestinian National Fund
Ḥāmid Abū Sittah	Independent	
ʻAbd al-Jawād Sāliḥ	Palestinian National Front	
†Dr Alfred Tūbāsī	Independent, of Christian origin, from Ramallah	
†Ḥabīb Qahwajī	Independent, of Christian origin, from Fasūtah	

*The dept of Affairs of the Occupied Homeland is run by a committee headed by Ḥāmid Abū Sittah, and whose members are Sāliḥ, Tūbāsi, Qahwajī and Abū Maizar.
†Not a member of the former EC.

The West Bank and Gaza Strip

ELIE REKHESS and DAN AVIDAN

POLITICAL DEVELOPMENTS IN THE WEST BANK

Lacking an independent political power base of their own, West Bankers for the last eleven years have had no control over developments affecting the Palestinian issue either in the international or inter-Arab arena. Since the beginning of Israeli rule in the area in 1967, local political activity and opinion have been determined by the relative stature of the three main political forces directly concerned—Israel, Jordan and the PLO. Fluctuations in the relative positions of Jordan and the PLO in the West Bank have been clearly discernible and have corresponded directly with the changes in their relative strength internationally and in the Arab world.

The growing international recognition of the PLO as the sole representative of the Palestinians (which accelerated after the Arab summit conference in Rabat in October 1974) proved to be among the PLO's main assets in its competition with Jordan in 1975-76 for the allegiance of the West Bankers. The West Bank municipal election results of April 1976 clearly reflected this upsurge of PLO influence. In many towns the National blocs—representing radical candidates, PLO supporters, communists and former members of the Arab Nationalist parties—won a decisive victory. In Hebron, for example, Fahd Qawāsimī replaced Shaykh Muḥammad 'Alī Ja'barī, a traditional leader known for his favourable views towards Jordan. In Nablus, Bassām Shak'a replaced Ḥājj Ma'zūz al-Masrī, a wealthy businessman who had close ties with the Hashemite regime. In Ramallah and Tulkarm, mayors Karīm Khalaf and Ḥilmī Ḥanūn (both staunch PLO supporters) were re-elected.

However, in the latter half of 1976, when the tide in Lebanon turned against the PLO, its position in the West Bank was considerably weakened. At the same time, Jordan's position in the Arab world was steadily enhanced, as indicated by the close relations established between Jordan and Syria.

JORDANIAN-PLO RIVALRIES

These developments provided Jordan with an opportunity to reassert its position and intensify its efforts to become more deeply involved in West Bank affairs. Having watched the performance of the new mayors, Jordan officially recognized the results of the West Bank municipal elections in late July 1976. Jordan's Minister of Information, 'Adnān Abū 'Awda, chairman of the governmental "Committee for the Occupied Territories' Affairs", congratulated the newly-elected mayors and invited them to Amman to discuss the resumption of financial aid, which Jordan had cut off shortly before the elections. The new mayors soon came to realize that committed though they were to the PLO on an ideological level, they nevertheless depended to a large extent on the financial assistance and co-operation of both the Israeli and Jordanian authorities. In fact, the necessity to cover municipal deficits prompted some local mayors to accept the invitation to visit Amman. The first to arrive was Mayor Fahd Qawāsimī in August 1976, followed late in the year by the mayors of Jericho, Bethlehem, al-Bīra, 'Anabtā, Salfīt and Bīr Zayt.

Mayor Qawāsimī's visit to Jordan occurred just when the Syrian-Palestinian confrontation in Lebanon reached its peak. To fend off PLO criticism of "collaboration" with Jordan, he stressed that the visit had no political significance and was devoted solely to solving economic and social problems. He also maintained that the financial support promised to Hebron did not imply any political or ideological commitment to Jordan. However, Jordanian aid was demonstratively withheld from those municipalities whose mayors declined to visit Amman. Thus, the question of financial assistance clearly served as a means of pressuring West Bank mayors to co-operate with Jordan.

These visits were also significant indicators of the decline in the PLO's influence in the West Bank. In this atmosphere, a number of the mayors not too firmly committed to the PLO—like those of Hebron, Qalqiliya and Jericho—made statements favouring future ties between the West Bank and Jordan on the basis of equality. They agreed that the West Bank should not be under direct Jordanian rule, but did not rule out King Ḥusayn's federation concept. Upon his return from Amman in late October 1976, Mayor Suwaytī of Jericho said that "Jordan is responsible for the West Bank"; the relationship between Jordan and the West Bank should be maintained because of "blood, language, and traditional ties with Jordan."[1] Defending his visit, Mayor Qawāsimī stressed that a distinction had to be made between ties with the Hashemite dynasty and ties with Jordan.

Jordan's pressure on the mayors was only partially successful in that the three most prominent PLO supporters—Karīm Khalaf of Ramallah, Ḥilmī Ḥanūn of Tulkarm and Bassām Shak'a of Nablus—refused to travel to Amman. Khalaf maintained in November that if the Jordanians were ready "to give us money without conditions . . . we will take it. But we cannot give our loyalty to the Jordanian regime, because our loyalty is to the PLO, to our people . . . to our country, Palestine."[2] Failing to persuade all the mayors, Jordan extended its efforts to groups other than municipalities, such as members of the Supreme Muslim Council, the Chambers of Commerce or labour associations; and to prominent pro-Jordanian personalities, such as Anwar al-Khatīb, the former Governor of Jerusalem, and Shaykh Muḥammad 'Alī Ja'barī, the former mayor of Hebron.

Ja'barī visited Amman in late 1976 and the beginning of 1977, for the first time since the 1967 war. He declared that the cohesion between the Jordanian and Palestinian peoples was historically inevitable, and that the Rabat summit resolutions could not revoke those of the 1948 Jericho Congress, under which the Palestinians themselves had opted for a merger of the West Bank with Transjordan.[3] These resolutions, he added, could be altered only by the Jordanian Parliament and Government, not by the PLO or by Arab summits. He stressed that it was the people of the West Bank—not the PLO—who should have the final say on the future of the territories, and called for the establishment of a new Palestinian party: "The Party of the Land." This would not necessarily replace the PLO, but would certainly be separate from it.

Even before his trip to Amman, Ja'barī suggested that the time had come to exclude the PLO from the political process which would determine the fate of the West Bank. In October 1976, he stated that as long as there was a body called the PLO, which behaved in the way it did, there would be no solution to the Palestinian question. The PLO, he said, must be courageous and realistic enough to admit that it had failed. "The PLO is incapable of negotiating . . . [It] wrought havoc in Jordan and now it is destroying Lebanon. It would do the same here [in the West Bank] given the chance . . . The [West Bank] people should authorize Jordan to negotiate on its behalf, so that afterwards [the people] will have the opportunity for self-determination."[4]

President Sādāt's statement in late December 1976 on the necessity of establishing formal links between Jordan and a future Palestinian state, and Arab pressures on the PLO to reach some form of reconciliation with Jordan, were signs to West Bankers that Jordan was regaining its position in the Arab world as a party directly involved in determining the political fate of the Palestinians. These external developments encouraged Jordanian efforts to strengthen its influence in the West Bank, and had a marked impact on West Bank political thinking. This was reflected in two ways: by the increasing self-confidence and more explicit expressions of support for Jordan in pro-Hashemite circles; and by the evident uneasiness felt by PLO supporters.

Commenting on Sādāt's statement, the East Jerusalem daily *al-Quds* (known for its favourable views towards Jordan) defined the nature of relations between the Jordanians and the Palestinians as "a geographical, historical, social and economic fusion."[5] It maintained that the concept of a Palestinian state linked with Jordan illustrated the Kingdom's important role in peace negotiations, as it provided an answer to Israel's refusal to accept a third [Palestinian] state between her and Jordan, thus removing an obstacle to Israeli withdrawal from the West Bank. A similar view was expressed in an article published in late January 1977 by Muḥammad 'Isā Dūdīn, a relative of Mustafā Dūdīn (for whose role, see below). He, too, argued that reliance on Jordan would provide the only way to terminate the Israeli occupation. "The problem since 1967 is not who will represent us [*man yumaththilunā*], but rather who will liberate us [*man yukhallisunā*] . . . The Rabat resolutions should be amended without delay to confer on the confrontation states responsibility for regaining the occupied territories . . . our fate, future and survival are dependent upon our iron-clad unity with Jordan."[6]

Another Hashemite sympathizer, Mayor Elias Freij of Bethlehem, warmly welcomed Sādāt's proposal. He expressed his belief that, following the establishment of a Palestinian state, "the majority of West Bankers will support a federation with Jordan on a basis of equality. . . . Jordan is our country, the people of Jordan are our people, and setting up such a federation will serve the interest of all."[7] Commenting on the process of reconciliation between Jordan and the PLO, Mayor Freij declared that the PLO had no choice but to "bow" to West Bank pressure for the revival of a reunion with Amman. He concluded that the establishment of close links with Jordan was "imperative."[8]

Pro-PLO leaders, on the other hand, responded uneasily to Sādāt's statement. Refraining from any open criticism of the Egyptian president, and asserting their commitment to the idea of Arab unity, they nevertheless stressed that the first priority was to establish an independent Palestinian state. Only thereafter, explained Bassām Shak'a, the mayor of Nablus, "shall we decide whether it is in our interest to unite with Jordan."[9]

An attempt by pro-PLO mayors to organize a delegation to meet UN Secretary-General Waldheim during his visit to Israel in February 1977 was reportedly frustrated by influential pro-Hashemite figures. Although this may have reflected growing pro-Jordanian influence, other events at the time proved that Jordanian gains remained limited. The city of Nablus, for instance, responded to a PLO appeal to stage a one-day protest strike on 10 February during Waldheim's visit in Israel. Furthermore, 14 local mayors, known for their PLO leanings, published a joint communiqué addressed to Waldheim in which they reasserted their loyalty to the PLO as the sole representative of the Palestinian people.

THE 13TH PALESTINIAN NATIONAL CONGRESS (PNC)

After overcoming numerous difficulties within the PLO and problems in its relations with Arab governments, the PNC convention opened in March 1977 in Cairo. The meeting had a marked effect on the population's attitude toward the

PLO, arousing high expectations in the West Bank and Gaza Strip, and was regarded as a turning point in the PLO's efforts to re-establish its inter-Arab and international standing. Even political personalities favourable to Jordan generally shared the mood of optimism expressed by West Bank PLO supporters. They, too, endorsed the view that the PLO should play a major role in any future Middle East negotiations, but urged the PNC to adopt a more realistic and flexible position to ensure the participation of Palestinians in future Arab peace efforts. The stance of the pro-Jordanians was illustrated by Mayor Freij's call to the PNC to adapt the Palestinian National Covenant to "the realities of 1977."[10]

The local press, while referring to the convention as a "fateful event", took the opportunity to express guarded criticism of the present PLO leadership and to call for enlarged West Bank and Gaza Strip representation in the PNC in order to lend greater substance and validity to its resolutions. Some PLO supporters in the West Bank shared the view that "after the tragedy in Lebanon we began to feel that the PLO no longer had a political line. We now hope that [the PNC] will give rise to new young elements that will clarify the line."[11] This indicated less than complete confidence that the PNC would, in fact, adopt resolutions likely to prove both timely and favourable to the West Bankers themselves.

Mayor Karīm Khalaf of Ramallah, representing a more radical point of view, urged the PNC to reject all US peace proposals, to increase co-operation with the Soviet Union, and to oppose a PLO-Jordanian *rapprochement*. Khalaf's insistence on increased reliance on the USSR reflected his close link to the Soviet-oriented Palestine National Front (PNF) in the West Bank.[12] The PNF sent a detailed memorandum to the PNC convention in which it strongly attacked "pro-American and reactionary Arab policy."[13] It stressed the need to end total Arab reliance on the US. In accordance with the basic guidelines of Soviet Middle East policy, the Front urged the PNC not to rule out the opportunity of PLO participation in Geneva since, in the PNF's view, political efforts carried no less weight than military struggle.

A number of West Bank mayors had been invited to attend the PNC meetings, but were not permitted to do so by the Military Government. However, all 24 West Bank mayors reportedly expressed their full support to the PLO in a memorandum. They conveyed their greetings to the convention, declared that they were rallying behind the PLO and pledged unity with its "loyal revolutionary leadership."[14] PLO sources said another petition sent by 7,000 "nationalist personalities in the occupied homeland"[15] authorized the PNC to adopt any measures that would ensure Israeli withdrawal from all territories occupied in 1967. It supported the establishment of an independent Palestinian state and called for the return of the 1948 refugees.

When the PNC meeting concluded, it was clear that 'Arafāt's leadership of the PLO had been maintained. West Bank support for the PLO was also reaffirmed, as that organization appeared to be overcoming the after-effects of the Lebanese crisis. The final PNC resolutions were enthusiastically welcomed by the West Bank press, radical and moderate alike. *Al-Quds*, for example, said the Palestinian leadership had "proved it is capable of bearing responsibility in these fateful times." It added that "the people of the occupied territories support any positive move that comes from the PNC, despite the fact that they didn't participate in its deliberations for known reasons."[16]

THE QUESTION OF EXTERNAL FUNDS

The PNC's resolutions on the West Bank and the Gaza Strip marked an increased PLO effort to strengthen its ties with the local population, as well as to offset Jordan's attempt to use economic aid as a means of leverage over the mayors. One of the resolutions stressed the importance of providing "comprehensive support for the various national institutions" in the territories, and called for the establishment of a financial fund to support "the people's steadfastness in the occupied homeland."[17] The PLO was thus endeavouring to exploit the fact that since March 1976, Jordan had failed to transfer financial assistance to West Bank municipalities. Although the newly-elected mayors who visited Jordan were promised aid, no funds had actually been transferred. The PLO was apparently anxious to supply direct assistance to the local municipalities from Arab sources not controlled by Ḥusayn and to reduce their dependence on Israeli grants.

In the spring of 1977, the Arab League adopted an aid programme to the West Bank and Gaza Strip municipalities, apparently in response to PLO proposals. Several cities in oil-rich Arab countries were twinned with West Bank and Gaza Strip towns. Following up this initiative, West Bank and Gaza Strip mayors toured Saudi Arabia, the United Arab Emirates, Kuwait, Libya and other Arab countries, where they were reportedly promised large sums of money. PLO patronage over these fund-raising visits was quite apparent: its representatives met the visiting delegations upon their arrival, arranged their schedules, and accompanied them at formal meetings. There were conflicting reports about the amount of money actually raised. Upon their return, the mayors reported that they had collected a total of c. $30m. However, as this money was deposited in banks in Amman and could not be withdrawn without Jordanian approval, Jordan frustrated the PLO plan and preserved its control over funds to the municipalities.

Israel also had every interest in preventing funds going to the municipalities if they in any way enhanced PLO influence in the area. Nevertheless, Defence Minister Ezer Weizman indicated that the new government was not opposed, in principle, to development projects in the West Bank and Gaza Strip being financed with outside aid. Finance Minister Simha Ehrlich further maintained in August that the Treasury had agreed to grant financial incentives to encourage the mobilization of funds from abroad for the improvement of municipal services in the West Bank.

PALESTINIAN ATTITUDES TO PEACE NEGOTIATIONS

The gains made by Jordan and its West Bank supporters in the first half of 1977 proved to be only of a limited and transitory nature and a product of tactical manoeuvres by Egypt, Syria and Saudi Arabia. In the long-run, however, none of these states revealed any readiness substantially to invalidate the Rabat resolutions which had designated the PLO as the sole legitimate representative of the Palestinian people.

Although West Bank support for the PLO had been eroded somewhat in late 1976 and early 1977, it began to gather strength again later in the year, paralleling the PLO's success in improving its position in the Arab world particularly after the PNC convention in March. The new trend in US policy which began to emerge in August and September 1977 also tilted the balance toward the PLO in the West Bank. The US aim—somehow to incorporate the PLO into the peace-making process—made it more difficult for the PLO's opponents to build up support.

The gathering momentum in the diplomatic process towards a Middle East settlement, as signified by the US Secretary of State's visit to the area in August, prompted an increased measure of political activity by both pro-PLO and pro-Jordanian supporters in the West Bank. Nine (pro-PLO) West Bank mayors addressed a memorandum to Secretary Vance which was said to have been delivered via the US Consulate in East Jerusalem. The mayors stated that the Arab Palestinian people were one indivisible unit and that the PLO, under Yāsir 'Arafāt's leadership was their sole legitimate representative. They maintained that any effort to disregard the PLO was pointless as well as a threat to peace; the Arab Palestinian people had the full right to establish their own independent and fully sovereign state; any attempt to impose links with any Arab or non-Arab country before the establishment of an independent Palestinian state would constitute a violation of the Palestinian people's rights. The mayors concluded that once the state had been set up, the people would be in a position to establish links with anyone they chose, in complete freedom and according to their own wishes. It is noteworthy that Mayor Freij of Bethlehem declined to sign the memorandum. At the time of Vance's visit to Israel, he was attending King Ḥusayn's Silver Jubilee ceremonies in Amman.

At a reception given by Foreign Minister Moshe Dayan in Tel Aviv on 11 August, the US Secretary of State briefly conferred with a group of prominent West Bank figures who presented him with two detailed memoranda reflecting a different line of thinking. The pro-PLO mayors had rejected Dayan's invitation to attend the reception. One memorandum was presented by ʻAzīz Shiḥāda, a prominent Ramallah lawyer, neither pro-Jordanian, nor a staunch supporter of the PLO. It called for the following:

1) Israelis and Palestinians should mutually recognize the legitimate rights of both peoples to sovereign national statehood in the land which both claim as their homeland.
2) A plebiscite should be held, possibly to be conducted during an interim period—when a "Peace-Promoting Force" acceptable to both Israelis and Palestinians might be needed—to enable the people of the West Bank and the Gaza Strip "to decide freely if they want to join with Jordan" or to set up "their own democratic Palestinian state, which we believe they will. We, the Palestinians, believe that our future lies with the Arab world and particularly with Jordan", but any such link would have to be achieved "by agreement with King Ḥusayn and the Hashemite Kingdom of Jordan", and not offered as a "ready-made solution."[18]
3) A non-aggression pact between Israel and the proposed Palestinian state should be reached as a first step towards closer relations.
4) Negotiated boundaries should be established, open to free passage and free movement of citizens of both states.
5) Shared sovereignty for Jerusalem should be realized through the creation of separate municipalities with a joint central committee.

More pronounced views on a desired linkage to Jordan were presented to Secretary Vance on the same occasion by the former mayor of Hebron, Shaykh Muḥammad ʻAlī Jaʻbarī (represented by his son, Burhān), and Mustafā Dūdīn. In his memorandum, Jaʻbarī stated that "the shortest line for a [Middle East] solution is the line connecting us [in the West Bank] with Amman."[19] He praised the co-operation between the West Bank and Jordan which had existed ever since the Jericho Congress in 1948, stressing his conviction that most Palestinians support a "Jordanian solution" which would ensure the security of Israelis and prevent communist infiltration to the area. Mustafā Dūdīn, a Hebronite who formerly served in several Jordanian cabinets, similarly suggested to Secretary Vance that the least complicated solution to the Middle East conflict would be an immediate return of the West Bank to Jordan.

During Vance's visit to Israel, a delegation of West Bank mayors and dignitaries were in Amman to participate in King Ḥusayn Silver Jubilee ceremonies. These included among others the mayors of Bethlehem, Bayt Sāḥūr, Bīr Zayt and Silwād. The mayors of Nablus, Tulkarm, Ramallah and Hebron had rejected Ḥusayn's invitation, reportedly on instructions from the PLO.

One of the prominent participants in Ḥusayn's celebrations was Ḥusayn al-Shuyūkhī, a Hebron lawyer residing in Ramallah. Upon his return to the West Bank in mid-August, Shuyūkhī initiated an overt anti-PLO campaign. While accepting in principle that the PLO was the sole representative of the Palestinians, he distinguished between the organization as such and its leadership, headed by Yāsir 'Arafāt, which he described as dictatorial, totalitarian and corrupt. Shuyūkhī blamed 'Arafāt for making a fortune at the expense of the Palestinians and and for failing to safeguard Palestinian interests. In spite of these views, Shuyūkhī denied any contact with the United Front of the Palestinian Forces (*jabhat al-quwwāt al-filastiniyya al-muttaḥida*) which distributed leaflets in the West Bank in late August depicting 'Arafāt as proclaiming himself "divine."[20] The leaflets blamed 'Arafāt for making a fortune at the expense of the Palestinians and challenged him to prove that he belonged to the Arab Palestinian people.

Shuyūkhī also challenged the PLO claim to be the sole representative of the Palestinians in the West Bank and Gaza Strip, maintaining that all Palestinians, and particularly the majority residing in the territories, should be given the right to participate in determining their fate. "We are not a flock of sheep, whose fate should be determined by a man ['Arafāt] who does not even own a house in the West Bank and who has no brother in this area so that he can feel what we feel."[21] Shuyūkhī further maintained that under the present circumstances, Palestinian interests could best be advanced "by leaving it to the Arab states to act for a peaceful solution . . . I am against any Palestinian going to Geneva. Those who sit around the negotiating table should be those who participated in the war [against Israel]. An independent Palestinian delegation at Geneva would absolve the Arab states of all their responsibilities and commitments towards the Palestinian people."[22] In fact, Shuyūkhī was implicitly preparing the ground for Jordan to re-assume responsibility toward the Palestinians (in particular those of the West Bank) and represent their interests at a future Geneva conference. It later became apparent that Shuyūkhī's initiative was actually backed by Jordan.

Shuyūkhī claimed that his views were widely shared by many West Bankers. However the only prominent figure to publicly support some of his ideas, though denying any formal link, was Mustafā Dūdīn, a member of the group that conferred in mid-August with Secretary Vance in Tel-Aviv. Dūdīn explicitly stated that the PLO had no rights whatsoever to represent the interests of the Palestinians in the territories. He reiterated his call for the return of the West Bank to Jordan, and disclosed in late September that a West Bank delegation was being organized for the purpose of travelling to the Arab countries to demand that responsibility for a settlement in the West Bank be restored to Jordan. However, such anti-PLO campaigns initiated in August and September 1977 failed to attract widespread public support in the West Bank, and Shuyūkhī's claim to represent a large faction of the local population remained unsubstantiated.

This failure should be interpreted in terms of the political atmosphere which prevailed in the area in late 1977. Secretary Vance's visit to the Middle East in August—followed by President Carter's meetings with the Israeli and Arab Foreign Ministers in the US in September and October—all marked the intensification of American efforts to accelerate the peace-making process and reconvene the Geneva conference. It became increasingly apparent that American policy supported the incorporation of the PLO, in one way or another, in any future peace negotiations. As lawyer 'Azīz Shihāda stated on 17 September, at a time when the PLO enjoyed international recognition as the sole representative of the Palestinians, "the West Bank could not espouse an anti-PLO stance."[23]

One of the issues raised within the framework of American diplomatic efforts in late 1977 was the question of a West Bank and Gaza Strip delegation to participate at Geneva. Israeli and American proposals that a non-PLO delegation of mayors and dignitaries should represent the Palestinians as part of a unified Arab delegation, or within the framework of a Jordanian-Palestinian delegation, aroused general criticism in the West Bank and further illustrated pro-PLO attitudes there at that time.

The local mayors adopted a unified stand, rejecting the notion of a separate West Bank and Gaza Strip delegation. They reiterated their oft-repeated argument that they were not authorized to negotiate political issues. As the mayor of Nablus remarked: "We did not receive a mandate from the people to negotiate the creation of a Palestinian state; the elections were held for the municipal councils only. We are not here as a substitute for the PLO, and we do not represent the whole of the Palestinian people."[24] In late September, the West Bank mayors addressed a memorandum to both Geneva co-chairmen, US Secretary of State Cyrus Vance and Soviet Foreign Minister Andrei Gromyko. They asserted that the PLO under 'Arafāt's leadership was the sole legitimate representative of the Palestinian people, and that any efforts to solve the issue without its participation would be fruitless.

Ḥilmī Ḥanūn, the mayor of Tulkarm, expressed a slightly different viewpoint. He said that if the PLO agreed to the inclusion of some mayors in the PLO delegation, "we would have no objection." Ḥanūn added that going to Geneva on the basis of UN Resolution 242 was totally unacceptable to the West Bankers as it "narrows the scope of the problem . . . We are a nation, we have the right to live as such . . . Treating us as refugees means that we shall continue to live in the area under Israeli occupation."[25]

Other West Bank voices, mainly from pro-Jordanian circles, argued that insistence upon an exclusive PLO presence in Geneva could lead to the reconvening of the peace conference with no Palestinian representation at all. In this case, they feared, Israel could possibly reach a peace agreement with the Arab states ignoring the Palestinian question altogether. To prevent this from happening, they insisted that the Palestinians should ensure their representation in Geneva—whatever the political framework proposed.

RELATIONS BETWEEN THE MILITARY GOVERNMENT AND THE LOCAL POPULATION

The municipal elections held in the West Bank in April 1976 substantially changed the relationship between Military Government authorities and the newly elected mayors. Many of the latter—PLO supporters known for their militant attitude towards the Israeli Administration—soon found themselves confronted with a difficult dilemma. They realized that in order to function efficiently and implement their election campaign promises, they had to come to terms with the Military Government. At the same time, having portrayed themselves as part of a new and militant municipal leadership, and being ideologically committed to the PLO, they had an interest in arousing unrest directed against the authorities in response to PLO appeals. The mayors' involvement in the organization of disorders in the West Bank in the summer of 1976 clearly indicated that during the period immediately following the elections, they opted for confrontation rather than search for a *modus vivendi* with the Military Government.

UNREST DUE TO THE IMPLEMENTATION OF VAT

The decision of the Israeli authorities in late June 1976 to apply Value Added Tax (VAT) to the West Bank and Gaza Strip—introduced shortly before in Israel—gave rise to disturbances and clashes between military forces and demonstrators in July and August. The local press strongly opposed the implementation of VAT, claiming that Israel not only intended to impoverish the West Bank by drawing off local capital from the area, but also to reinforce the *de facto* annexation of the territories. The mayors' efforts to mount a sustained protest was supported (mainly by means of radio appeals) by the PLO which depicted it as a show of PLO solidarity. Jordan also saw an opportunity to exploit signs of opposition to the Israeli occupation as a means of promoting its own nationalist posture in the eyes of the local population.

The disturbances revealed another important aspect of the pattern of political behaviour in the West Bank; namely, the divergence of interest between the new mayors and the leaders of the Chambers of Commerce. The latter displayed a relatively moderate attitude and demanded an end to the August 1976 strike, which paralysed business activity in the West Bank for three weeks. Obviously they were motivated by economic considerations and acted under pressure from major businessmen in the West Bank. On the other hand, the new mayors (most of whom did not belong to the business community) could afford to call for continued agitation and so fortify their "nationalist image."

A period of relative quiet followed the Defence Ministry's decision to postpone the implementation of VAT until early December 1976. At the end of this interim period, however, disturbances broke out again. Commercial and school strikes were organized in almost all West Bank towns. Road blocks were set up, tyres burnt and rocks hurled. In Qalandiya, a 15-year old boy was wounded when shots were fired by security forces dispersing demonstrators. In the wake of the riot attempts, curfews were imposed in Nablus, Ramallah and Qalqiliya. Once again, the unrest was promoted by the more radical among the newly-elected mayors; namely, Bassām Shak'a of Nablus and Karīm Khalaf of Ramallah. However, following a compromise reached between the Military Government and the West Bank Chambers of Commerce, the local population as well as the mayors resigned themselves to the implementation of the tax. According to the compromise, all but 1,500 to 2,000 prominent businessmen earning over IL 500,000 a year were exempted from the bookkeeping work involved in VAT payments.

In contrast to the stormy events in the latter part of 1976, a period of relative quiet descended over the West Bank in 1977. Civil protest on a rather limited scale was occasionally organized, but soon subsided. Such was the case until mid-March 1977 when the PNC convention in Cairo became the occasion for student demonstrations in support of the PLO. Trade and school strikes were also held in most West Bank towns in late March 1977 to mark the first anniversary of "The Day of the Land."

As in previous years, the Jewish settlements' issue continued to stir up resentment in the West Bank. In April 1977, disturbances broke out in Nablus following attempts by Rabbi Meir Kahana to lay the cornerstone for a new settlement near the town. A month later, two inhabitants of Qabatiyya were killed by IDF soldiers during demonstrations against alleged attempts by Gush Emunim to settle at a nearby location. However, after the Israeli general elections in May 1977 until the end of October, there were no large-scale manifestations of civil unrest in the West Bank (see below).

STRICTER CONTROLS BY THE MILITARY AUTHORITIES

A major reason for the relative calm which prevailed in the West Bank during 1977 seemed to be the more resolute policy adopted by Military Government authorities in dealing with the local municipal leadership. The stricter Israeli policy was apparently a direct reaction to the militant stand taken by some of the more radical mayors in the latter part of 1976 and was possibly calculated to weaken their positions (especially in Nablus and Ramallah). One of the new preventive measures taken by the Military Government was the permanent stationing of military forces inside West Bank towns (rather than being on call outside).

While the mayors persisted in their running confrontation, they nevertheless came to realize that their ability to organize future disorders had been severely hampered by the new policy adopted by the Military Government. Moreover, their experience clearly showed that to continue to foment disturbance would have little effect on that Government's determination to carry out its policies. The local population was coming to feel the accumulative impact of the upheavals. This was reflected in an editorial in *Al-Quds* (14 December 1976) which welcomed the Nablus municipality's efforts to restore normal life. It stressed that "destroying part of our country's economy and educational life does not harm the occupation as it does our cause . . . We must conduct ourselves with a clear mind, open to the events and the developments of the future without indulging in emotionalism."

Another reason for this relative quiet derived from the severe setback the PLO suffered in Lebanon and, more generally, as a result of the Lebanese civil war. Some PLO circles had hoped that precisely because of the developments in Lebanon, disturbances in the West Bank would continue and even intensify, so as to demonstrate Palestinian support for the PLO. A senior PLO official interviewed in Beirut in March 1977 confirmed that the PLO was encouraging West Bank dissent, hoping to keep it visible and voluble. "With the situation in Lebanon what it is, it makes sense to keep the protests and demonstrations going along in the West Bank."[26] In reality, though, the impact of the Lebanese crisis had the opposite effect.

Another factor contributing to the maintenance of quiet in the West Bank, particularly in the latter part of 1977, was the rise to power in Israel of the Likud. The new government's hawkish image apparently aroused apprehensions in some West Bank mayors and led them to decrease their involvement in organizing civil unrest. The willingness of local teachers and other educators to co-operate with the authorities also helped in preventing student demonstrations.

In spite of a notable decline in the level of civil disturbance in the West Bank in 1977, the Military Government's relations with some of the newly elected mayors was still characterized by substantial friction. The Military Government apparently tried to restrict the authority of the mayors to the performance of purely administrative municipal duties. Furthermore they were deprived of some prerogatives enjoyed by their predecessors, such as being consulted on appointments to local education departments. They were instructed not to interfere in family reunions or the granting of amnesties for political prisoners, and to discontinue visits to the prisons on religious occasions. Duties traditionally exercised by some of the mayors were assigned to others. For example, the mayor of Hebron was reportedly excluded from discussions over prayer arrangements in the Tomb of the Patriarchs. Instead, local religious dignitaries and ex-mayor Shaykh Ja'barī—who had been considered the local spokesman on this issue during his term of office—were consulted by the authorities. The Military Government also tried to strengthen public and municipal bodies, such as the Chambers of Commerce and the local education departments, in an effort to further weaken the influence of the mayors.

The Military Government's stricter policy elicited a sharp reaction in the East Jerusalem press. *Al-Quds* commented in March 1977 on the "iron-fist image of the Military Government." It added that there were reports from several municipalities about worsening relations between the mayors and some senior functionaries in the Military Government. "These functionaries have behaved in an unbecoming and irresponsible manner towards the municipalities in an effort to demonstrate the muscles of authority for no reason."[27]

The deterioration in relations between the authorities and the municipalities took various forms. For example, the Military Government delayed loans and grants to the municipalities; the West Bank mayors complained that "political" clauses were inserted into the loan contracts between the two sides. Such clauses stipulated that the Hebrew version of the contract was the binding one and that, in case of dispute, action would be brought in an Israeli court. Since the politically-minded mayors refused to accept such clauses, the process of transferring loans became more protracted. The departure of several pro-PLO mayors for a fund-raising mission in Arab states in the latter part of 1977 was also delayed on the grounds that the relevant municipal development plans had yet to be approved.

Another legal dispute with political overtones arose over the mayors' refusal to deduct increased income tax rates from municipal salaries in accordance with the recent reform of the Israeli internal revenue system. The Military Government countered by subtracting these sums from regular payments transferred to the municipalities while the mayors, in turn, refused to accept the cheques for smaller sums.

POLICY OF THE LIKUD GOVERNMENT

The election of the Likud government in May 1977 aroused expectations of a more forceful Israeli policy in the West Bank and Gaza Strip. However the new administration did not introduce any immediate changes in Israel's basic policy guidelines, as formulated in 1967.

In his capacity as the newly-appointed Minister of Defence, Ezer Weizman maintained that, as Israel did not intend to withdraw from the West Bank and the Gaza Strip, it should seek ways to coexist peacefully with the Arab population in the territories and try to minimize points of friction. This, he explained, meant allowing the local population greater latitude in handling their own civil affairs according to their religious and cultural traditions and their customary social principles.

In line with previous policies, he stressed the importance of tranquillity for economic prosperity. Weizman repeated on several occasions that peaceful coexistence between Israel and the populations of the West Bank and Gaza Strip could be achieved by assisting the local inhabitants to raise their standard of living.[28] Central to this policy was the mid-August Cabinet decision to raise the standard of public services (health, transportation, welfare) in the West Bank and Gaza Strip to that enjoyed in Israel. Most West Bank leaders viewed this decision as "one more step towards annexation" and labelled it as a "veiled move" aimed at integrating the territories with Israel. Mayor Qawāsimī of Hebron said that if the decision was aimed only at improving living conditions, it was welcome; but if the aim was to annex the territories to Israel, "we emphatically reject it."[29] However, by late October 1977, there were still no indications that the government had taken any practical steps to implement its decision.

POLITICAL DEVELOPMENTS IN THE GAZA STRIP

The pattern of relationships between the Military Government and the local population in the Gaza Strip, economic growth and general tranquillity which characterized the area 1976–77 all had their origins in the events of the previous decade.

In the period between 1967–71, the Palestinian organizations in the Gaza Strip succeeded in establishing numerous strongholds mainly in the densely-populated refugee camps, from where they carried out frequent sabotage operations either against Israeli forces or against targets in the local population. The organizations achieved a dominant basis of influence over the local inhabitants and were able to hamper the Military Government's efforts to normalize the situation. In that atmosphere, the local leadership proved reluctant to co-operate with the Israeli authorities. This attitude was exemplified by the behaviour of Rāghib al-'Alamī, the then mayor of Gaza, who refused to maintain a working relationship with the Military Government. During these four years of militant confrontation between the urban pro-PLO/pro-Egyptian leadership and the Military Government, a number of prominent figures were banished to Sinai for limited periods. But leaders with pro-Jordanian leanings or with a more co-operative attitude towards the authorities also failed to achieve any real positions of influence.

The beginning of 1971 marked a change in Israeli policy toward the Gaza Strip. After the removal of Mayor 'Alamī in early January, a sustained military campaign was launched against the PLO; their forces were almost entirely eliminated in the Gaza Strip, and their influence declined significantly. An integral part of the campaign was substantially to diminish the numbers of Palestinian forces in the highly-populated refugee camps, which had previously been their haven. Roads were built and electricity installed; refugees whose houses were demolished in this operation were offered alternative and better housing outside the camps. Subsequently, over the last three years, c. 3,000 refugee families have been resettled. This rehousing programme together with extensive employment opportunities in Israel contributed to a substantially higher standard of living of the entire Gaza population.[30] These developments, along with the general decline of the PLO's standing in the Arab world after its expulsion from Jordan in 1971, paved the way for a new relationship in the Strip between the Military Government and local leaders. Although there were occasional demonstrations over such issues as the imposition of the Value Added Tax (VAT), or over the condition of Arabs in Israeli prisons, these were of a limited nature. In general, the local population was reluctant to endanger its recently acquired economic prosperity by engaging in hostile activity. The result has been a prolonged period of relative calm.

Unlike the West Bank, where municipal elections were held in spring 1976, the municipal leadership in the Strip underwent no major changes. The Gaza mayoralty of Hājj Rashshād al-Shawā retained its influential position as a central political factor both in domestic politics and *vis-à-vis* the Military Government.

PRO-HASHEMITE VS PRO-PLO/PRO-EGYPTIAN ELEMENTS

Gaza politics continued to be dominated by historical and sociological divisions between a pro-Hashemite group and pro-PLO/pro-Egyptian elements. The latter drew most of their support from the more radical younger generation whose leaders were from the educated élite—mainly liberal professional men who, during the period of Egyptian rule, occupied key posts in the local administration. These included Dr Ḥaydar 'Abd al-Shāfī, a former member of the PLO Supreme Council in Gaza, and Ibrāhīm Abū Sitta, formerly a member both of the PLO Executive Committee and of the Egyptian-appointed Executive Council of Gaza. The pro-Hashemites came mainly from the older established generation, often defined as traditional or conservative. Many of them belonged to the business and commercial élite who benefited from the economic ties that developed between Jordan and Gaza after the June 1967 war. This group remained under the uncontested leadership of Mayor Rashshād al-Shawā, a wealthy citrus grower and prominent businessman, whose family has long-standing ties with the regime in Jordan. Shawā was appointed mayor of Gaza in September 1971, resigned in September 1972, but was reappointed in October 1975 and is still in office. Mainly through the services of the al-Shawā family, Jordan granted the Gaza Strip population economic and commercial concessions, such as permits for Gaza lorries to export agricultural produce to Jordan and other Arab countries via "open bridges" across the Jordan river.

With all political organizations banned, the rival Gaza groups channelled much of their activity into two local philanthropic societies. The Red Crescent Society, headed by Dr Ḥaydar 'Abd al-Shāfī and Ibrāhīm Abū Sitta, was identified as a PLO stronghold in Gaza, mainly involved in financing medical institutions and raising external Arab capital for economic investment in the area. Jordanian interests were represented by the Benevolent Society for the Welfare of the Gaza Strip Inhabitants. Directed by 'Abd al-Karīm al-Shawā, a relative of the Gaza mayor, this society functioned as a kind of consular agency for Amman. It granted one-month permits to Gazans who wished to travel to Arab countries via Jordan, and eleven-month permits to university students in Arab countries. It also approved shipments of citrus from Gaza to Jordan and verified Israel-issued certificates.

The pro-PLO/pro-Egyptian group frequently found ways of giving expression to its political orientation. Thus, at the end of 1976, when Egypt agreed to unfreeze the bank deposits of Gaza citrus growers (blocked in Cairo since 1967), Shaykh Furaykh al-Musaddar thanked President Sādāt and declared that all Gaza Strip residents would remain faithful to Egypt under his leadership. A Gaza delegation, whose members included Dr Ḥaydar 'Abd al-Shāfī, Ibrāhīm Abū Sitta and Maḥmūd Nijm, visited Egypt in January 1977 and was received by Sādāt and his Foreign Minister. The PLO's local representative, Jamāl Surānī (member of a well-known Gaza family) assumed the leadership of the delegation, which declared its support for Egypt, stressed Sādāt's role as leader of the Arab nations, and praised Egypt's contribution to the peacemaking process in the Middle East. It also re-affirmed its full support for the PLO under 'Arafāt's leadership and emphasized the need to co-ordinate the efforts of Egypt, Syria and the Palestinians in restoring Arab solidarity—pointedly omitting any mention of Jordan.

These pro-Egyptian manifestations were reflected in Cairo's renewed interest and greater involvement in Gaza. In March 1976, President Sādāt announced the reinstatement of the Gaza Strip Executive Council[31] with Ibrāhīm Abū Sitta named as Director for Civil Affairs. In January 1977, Sādāt appointed Vice-President Ḥusnī Mubārak to be in charge of Gaza Strip affairs, and instructed all Egyptian government agencies to respond immediately to applications from Gaza Strip residents, paying special regard to their education and labour needs. Egyptian consular delegations in Europe were also instructed to facilitate the provision of refugee *laissez-passez* documents to Gaza Strip residents. Later in the year, Egypt agreed to increase the quota of Gaza students to Egyptian universities and to pay pensions to Gazans previously employed by the Egyptian government.

One possible explanation for Egypt's greater attention to the Gaza Strip was that it wished to strengthen its base in the area at the expense of pro-Jordanian groups. Also, by strengthening its position in Gaza, Egypt could hope to extend its influence over the PLO and counter similar efforts by Syria.

While stressing their allegiance to Cairo, members of the pro-PLO/pro-Egyptian group repeatedly expressed support for the PLO as the sole legitimate representative of the Palestinian people. In March 1977, for example, shortly before the PNC convention in Cairo, Zuhayr al-Rayis, a known PLO sympathizer, declared that all Palestinians everywhere were united under the PLO leadership. He expressed support for 'Arafāt and rejected any attempt to change the PLO's status as the sole representative of the Palestinians until the goal of a Palestinian state had been achieved. Only then would it be possible to discuss the question of federative or unitary links with other Arab states. In October 1977, a group of 20 Gaza dignitaries sent a memorandum to the UN Secretary-General and the Arab League

Secretary-General reaffirming the PLO as the sole legitimate representative of the Palestinians, and demanding PLO participation in all discussions on the Palestinian problem. They added that the Gaza Strip was an indivisible part of Palestinian territory and its inhabitants inseparable from the Palestinian people. The memorandum was signed mainly by staunch PLO supporters such as Dr Ḥaydar 'Abd al-Shāfī, Ibrāhīm Abū Sitta and Fa'iz Abū Raḥma, but also by Mayor Rashshād al-Shawā.

THE ROLE OF GAZA'S MAYOR

Mayor Shawā, although basically pro-Jordanian, found it necessary throughout 1977 to express his commitment to the PLO, the strength of this commitment varying according to the relative positions of Jordan and the PLO in the inter-Arab and international arenas. At the beginning of 1977, following the PLO's defeat in Lebanon, Shawā often challenged its leaders by demanding larger representation for Palestinians in the PNC—from "wherever they are."

In the spring of 1977, Shawā embarked on a fund-raising mission to Abū Dhabī and Saudi Arabia. On his return, he announced that Abū Dhabī had responded with a $2m grant for Gaza's municipal services; Riyadh, named by the Arab League as twin city to Gaza, had promised to examine a $100m request for a five-year project. Shawā conceded that he had met with PLO officials in Damascus, and that the organization had assigned a special envoy to accompany him to Abū Dhabī. It was noteworthy, however, that during his fund-raising tour, Shawā stopped over in Amman where he conferred with Prime Minister Badrān, and where he also deposited the money reportedly collected in Abū Dhabī.

Shawā visited Jordan again in August at the head of a large delegation to participate in King Husayn's Jubilee ceremonies. (In February, after Queen 'Aliā's death, he had led a similar delegation to offer condolences to the King.) In Amman, Shawā reiterated his support for the PLO, but went on to praise the Jordanian regime for its efforts to "liberate the occupied territories."[32] He expressed Gaza's gratitude for Jordan's help to them to "face Israeli pressure." Progress towards terminating Israeli occupation, Shawā concluded, was conditional upon closer co-operation between Jordan and the PLO.

However, in October 1977, Shawā came out uncompromisingly in favour of PLO participation at Geneva. In response to Israeli and American proposals that the Palestinians should be represented at Geneva by a West Bank and Gaza Strip delegation, Shawā declared in October that "the PLO is our sole representative; the invitation to Geneva must come through the PLO; I cannot imagine that a reasonable Palestinian will go to Geneva without the nomination or the overt agreement of the PLO."[33]

Despite Shawā's periodic declarations of support for the PLO, his close ties with the Hashemite regime exposed him to vehement criticism from pro-PLO circles in Gaza, and particularly from the radical East Jerusalem paper, *al-Fajr*. Throughout 1976 and early 1977, he was attacked for having accepted the Military Government's appointment as mayor in 1975; for mishandling city affairs; for raising municipal taxes; and for implementing Military Government projects, allegedly intended to impose Israeli-controlled home rule in the Gaza Strip. However, the basic reason for such criticisms was Shawā's pro-Jordanian position.

In an attempt to counteract these accusations, Shawā urgently demanded municipal elections in February 1977. He explained that "we want to pursue the same course as the West Bank municipalities which held elections [in April 1976]. This is in order to co-ordinate the citizens in the West Bank and Gaza. . . . We do not want the people to say that we are an appointed municipal council."[34]

PLO broadcasts strongly attacked Shawā's proposal to hold elections, and coupled their criticism with an attack on his favourable stand toward Jordan. One PLO radio commentary read: "He [Shawā] . . . wants to hold elections that will guarantee his re-election as mayor by using bribes and favouritism and buying the conscience of some hesitant weak persons . . . imagining in advance his victory with the backing of the Zionist occupiers who usually supervise the ballot boxes . . . [he] placed himself at the disposal of the Zionist aggressive forces and drove away the nationalists and revolutionists, handing them over to the enemy."[35] The commentary added that Shawā's "political inclinations" tended towards a "well-known Arab side [i.e. Jordan], that opposes any kind of national sovereignty and independence for our Palestinian people . . . and this is contrary to all he utters about his alleged support of the PLO."

While not totally rejecting Shawā's proposal for holding elections, the Military Government replied that the issue involved complicated legislative arrangements and required a longer period of study, especially as elections had not been held in Gaza since 1946. Israeli sources suggested that because of the election results in the West Bank in 1976, the Military Government was anxious to avoid the possibility of a PLO candidate becoming mayor. In late March, Shawā withdrew his threat to resign. Manoeuvring with careful calculation between verbal commitments to the PLO and close and friendly ties with Jordan, Shawā succeeded in preserving his position as the most prominent and influential leader in the Gaza Strip.

NOTES

1. Israel Broadcasting Authority, 30 October—Daily Report (DR), 3 November 1976.
2. *The Guardian*, London; 16 November 1976.
3. The Jericho Congress had prepared the ground for Jordan's annexation of the West Bank in 1948.
4. *Yediot Aharonot*, Tel Aviv; 14 October 1976.
5. *Al-Quds*, East Jerusalem; 10 January 1977.
6. *Al-Anbā'*, Jerusalem; 25 January 1977.
7. *Al-Quds*, 24 January 1977.
8. *Jerusalem Post*, 26 January 1977.
9. *The Guardian*, 4 January 1977.
10. *Al-Sha'b*, East Jerusalem; 9 March 1977.
11. *Ibid.*
12. The PNF was established in the West Bank and in the Gaza Strip in late 1973 by members of the Jordanian Communist Party, ex-members of the Arab Nationalist Party and by supporters of the Palestinian organizations. The PNF regarded itself as an integral part of the PLO. It was recognized in 1974 by the PLO as its representative in the West Bank.
13. *Al-Ittihād*, Haifa; 18 March 1977.
14. Voice of Palestine, Radio Cairo, 14 March—British Broadcasting Corporation, Summary of World Broadcasts: the ME and Africa (BBC), 17 March 1977.
15. *Ibid.*
16. *Al-Quds*, 21 March 1977.
17. Voice of Palestine, Radio Cairo, 22 March—BBC, 25 March 1977.
18. *Jerusalem Post*, 12 August 1977.
19. *Ha'aretz*, Tel Aviv; 12 August 1977.
20. Israel Television, 24 August—BBC, 26 August 1977.
21. *Al-Anbā'*, 2 September 1977.
22. *Ibid.*
23. *Jerusalem Post*, 18 September 1977.
24. Quoted in A Sinai and A Pollack (eds.), *The Hashemite Kingdom of Jordan and the West Bank* (New York, 1977), p. 251.
25. *Ma'ariv*, Tel Aviv; 12 October 1977.
26. *The New York Times*, 23 March 1977.
27. *Al-Quds*, 19 March 1977.
28. Disposable *per capita* private income increased in the West Bank on the average, at constant prices, from IL 831 in 1967 to IL 1,365 in 1975. The planned investment by the

Military Government in building and road construction in the West Bank and the Gaza Strip in 1976–77 totalled IL 60m. Projects under construction included, *inter alia*, the extension of the Shifa Hospital in Gaza and the Rafidiya Hospital in Nablus, at a total investment of c. IL 45m. Government Press Office, *The Administered Territories —Background Data*, June 1977.

29. Israel Broadcasting Authority, 15 August—BBC, 17 August 1977.
30. Disposable *per capita* private income increased on the average, at constant prices, from IL 553 in 1967 to 1,158 in 1975. The percentage of families possessing TV sets rose from 3% in 1967 to 34% in 1976. *The Administered Territories, op cit.*
31. This body was originally set up by Egypt in 1962. It consisted of 13 members, five of whom were Palestinians, and the remainder Egyptians. All were appointed by the Egyptian Minister of War and were in charge of government departments.
32. *Al-Dustūr*, Amman; 12 August 1977.
33. *Al-Quds*, 3 October 1977.
34. *Al-Dustūr*, 17 February—DR, 18 February 1977.
35. Voice of Palestine, Radio Cairo, 15 February—DR, 17 February 1977. The broadcast was probably referring to an incident which occurred in November 1971 when Ziyyād al-Ḥusaynī, a leading commander of the PFLP in the Gaza Strip, committed suicide at Shawā's residence in Gaza, after hiding there for some weeks.

A Chronology and Commentary on Political Developments in the Arab-Israel Conflict (October 1976-October 1977)

MOSHE GAMMAR

THE ARAB "PEACE OFFENSIVE"

At the Riyadh summit meeting (16-18 October 1976) and at the Cairo meeting (26-28 October 1976), the leaders of Syria, Saudi Arabia and Egypt decided, in view of the approaching end of the US election year and consequently of the stalemate in the ME political process, to co-ordinate their positions and concentrate once more on the Arab-Israeli conflict. The Arab leaders reportedly agreed to end the Egyptian-Syrian rivalry by a compromise whereby Egypt undertook not to seek further separate agreements nor a separate peace with Israel; Syria would not interfere with Egyptian political activity in mounting a diplomatic and public peace offensive; and Saudi Arabia would apply quiet pressure on the US and help to strengthen Egypt's military capacity by the purchase of arms.

Carter's election in November 1976 caused concern among the Arabs because of the pro-Israeli stand he had taken during the election campaign. The Egyptian media called on Arab rulers to initiate immediate contacts with the President-elect to ensure that, after taking office, he would be more favourable to the Arabs.[1] A week after the elections, Egypt launched its "peace offensive." In a series of interviews and meetings with Western (especially US) media and political figures during the last months of 1976 and the beginning of 1977, Sādāt emphasized Egypt's readiness to sign a "peace agreement" which would be "a document, formally, legally and publicly ending the state of belligerency."[2] He declared that in order "to satsify its feeling of security," Israel could ask for and obtain any guarantees from anyone it wished—even a mutual defence pact between the US and Israel. Egypt would not object provided that such guarantees were given to it as well (Cairo would not ask for a defence treaty). Furthermore, it would not object to the stationing of UN forces or "whatever forces were agreed upon" on the borders and in Sharm al-Shaykh "to guarantee free shipping in the 'Aqaba Gulf." When asked about specific issues, such as the nature of peace or the Arab boycott, Sādāt answered that he was interested in dealing with the "big issues," while "the rest will be solved by themselves."[3] Through the mediation of the Austrian Chancellor, Bruno Kreisky, Sādāt tried to meet Jewish, and even Zionist leaders from the US. In mid-December 1976, a delegation of the US Zionist Organization, headed by its chairman Charlotte Jacobson, visited Cairo and met Sādāt. The visit received considerable publicity in the West, but was not mentioned in the Egyptian media.

The "peace offensive" was accompanied by warnings, especially in statements for internal consumption, that the military option remained in case diplomatic efforts failed; Arab media specifically warned of a possibility of war at the beginning of 1977. The "oil weapon" was mentioned by Saudi leaders on rare occasions, though more frequently by the Saudi press. In January 1977, the Saudi Foreign Minister, Sa'ūd al-Faysal, said: "By limiting the crude oil price rise, we are contributing to the stabilization of the Western economy. In return, we expect Europe and the US to show greater understanding of our arguments on the Palestinian conflict."

The "peace offensive" was largely successful in convincing Western opinion, especially in the US, of Egypt's sincere moderation and interest in peace. The then US Secretary of State, Dr Kissinger, said privately that Sādāt was "obviously a more courageous negotiator" than Prime Minister Rabin.[5] Carter, too, spoke of "the moderation of the Arab leaders" which, together with Israel's longing for peace, "give us hope that real achievements can be achieved in new negotiations between Israel and the Arabs."[6]

THE PLO LINE

As part of the peace offensive, Egypt and to some extent Saudi Arabia as well as circles within the PLO made an effort to present that organization as being ready to moderate its attitudes. During November 1976, PLO and Egyptian sources, especially Farūq al-Qaddūmī, head of the PLO's Political Department, hinted that the PLO might give some kind of recognition to Israel. Expectations were that the forthcoming Central Council (CC) meeting in Damascus, due in mid-December 1976, would decide on the issue. Such feelings were strengthened by the Chairman of the PLO Executive Committee, Yāsir 'Arafāt, who said that "a unified Palestine is my dream—and I have the right to dream," but that "we are prepared to establish an independent regime in any territory that we liberate or from which Israel withdraws."[7] When the CC did not decide on such a move, new expectations arose that the Palestine National Council (PNC), due to meet in Cairo in March 1977, would announce changes in its policy.

The meetings of PLO representatives with prominent figures in the Israeli Council for Israel-Palestine Peace and the Israeli Communist Party (Rakaḥ), also contributed to the moderate image of the PLO. However, these meetings were not official, and PLO spokesmen denied that they had taken place.

On 13 February 1977, the Vienna daily *Arbeiter-Zeitung* published 'Isām Sartāwi's letter of 26 January to Chancellor Kreisky, in which he stated that if a Palestinian state were to be set up in the West Bank, the Gaza sector and the Hamma and 'Awja enclaves, "a state of non-belligerency [could be] established between the new state and Israel." But "a state of peace" required other issues to be settled, the most important of which was Israeli acceptance and implementation of "the rights of the Palestinian refugees to return to their original homes," or the right to compensation for those not wishing to do so.[8] Again, the PLO promptly denied that the letter represented its views.

As the date of the PNC opening (12 March) drew closer, PLO spokesmen emphasized that they regarded the "mini-state" as only a first step towards the PLO's ultimate goal—the "democratic secular state of Palestine." In spite of pressure for moderation, the PNC decided to reject Resolution 242 and all "American capitulationist settlements," and to continue, "without any conciliation or recognition" of Israel, the struggle for "the national rights of our people, in particular the rights to return, self-determination and establishing an independent national state on [our] soil."[9]

ISRAELI RESPONSE TO THE "PEACE OFFENSIVE"

Initially, Israel's official spokesmen dismissed the "peace offensive" as mere propaganda, but found it hard to counteract the image of an "inflexible Israeli attitude" as against "Arab moderation" in the Western, and especially US, public mind and media.

From the end of November 1976 onwards Israel began to challenge the moderate image of Sādāt by initiating proposals of her own. Among these were calls by Allon and Rabin to their Egyptian counterparts, Fahmī and Sādāt, for direct meetings "at any time and in any place"; at the Socialist International Congress in Geneva on 27 November, Rabin suggested that the Geneva conference be turned into a "Helsinki conference of the ME problem." [10] Shimòn Peres proposed in January 1977 to establish either a West Bank-Israel federation or a Jordan-West Bank-Israel confederation. [11] For the first time, Israel also submitted a draft resolution at the UN General Assembly during the debate on the situation in the ME (see essay, "The UN and the Arab-Israeli Conflict"). However, Israel's efforts apparently did not succeed in improving its image or in discrediting Sādāt's; Allon's and Rabin's suggestions were rejected by Egypt as "propaganda gimmicks."

ARAB LEADERS CO-ORDINATE THEIR POSITIONS

Shortly before Carter's inauguration on 20 January 1977, the Arab states participating in the political process—Saudi Arabia, Egypt, Syria and Jordan—tried to co-ordinate their tactics and policies. In a series of meetings between Sādāt and Asad (18–21 December 1976), Sādāt and Ḥusayn (13–15 January 1977), and the Foreign Ministers of the "Confrontation" states, the Arabian peninsula oil-producing states and representatives of the PLO (in Riyadh, 9–10 January and in Cairo, 15 January 1977), the four countries reportedly agreed to a united strategy for 1977. This was: 1) to put pressure on the new US administration, mainly through Saudi Arabia; 2) to try to reconvene the Geneva conference during the first half of 1977; 3) to exert pressure on the PLO so that the PNC meeting (due in March 1977) would moderate its attitudes and declare its readiness to establish a Palestinian mini-state in the West bank and the Gaza Strip; and 4) to allow Jordan some status on the Palestinian question. (Since the Rabat 1974 summit resolution, Jordan's only claim to participation in the Geneva conference was through its role as a Confrontation state.)

At the end of December 1976, Sādāt declared that a Palestinian state should have formal links with Jordan. [12] In early January 1977, he added that the relationship had to be agreed upon by Ḥusayn and the PLO. [13] Fahmī said that while it was up to Jordan and the PLO, Egypt would "encourage a link between them." [14]

At the Sādāt-Ḥusayn talks on 13–15 January 1977, both sides referred to the Palestinians as having a right "to set up an independent political entity," and to Jordan only as a Confrontation state. However, Ḥusayn expressed "Jordan's welcome . . . for establishing very close relations with the Palestinian state which will be set up . . . the form of [which] . . . will be decided by the two peoples through their free choice, proceeding from the unity of purpose and fate and the complete identity of interests and feeling." [15] Sādāt said that the Palestinians should have their own delegation at the Geneva conference "but linked by some way or another with the Jordanian delegation." [16] He was thus trying to ease in advance the complications he anticipated over the question of Palestinian representation.

Asad, too, indicated that he would support a Palestinian mini-state linked with Jordan. He said further that if the PLO refused to participate in the Geneva conference, "we will not exert pressure on them"; however, "the movement of the Arab states towards a settlement will not be paralysed." [17]

THE ELECTION CAMPAIGN IN ISRAEL

While the Arab leaders were busy co-ordinating their policy, Israel remained preoccupied with internal affairs. On 20 December 1976, Rabin submitted his (and consequently his government's) resignation and announced the decision to bring forward the elections, due in November 1977, "to the earliest possible date." These were later fixed for 17 May 1977.

The election campaign, preceded by Rabin's resignation as candidate for the Premiership and his subsequent replacement by Shimon Peres in April 1977, had no effect—declared or practical—on Arab and American policies. Israel continued to react to American and Arab moves, rather than to promote new initiatives. However, there was one notable exception. The Labour Party's convention decided on 25 February to change its former position of offering territorial concessions in exchange for peace, to an offer of concessions "on all frontiers" (i.e. including the West Bank). After the former Defence Minister Moshe Dayan (who had been known for his opposition to concessions in the West Bank) threatened to leave the party, Rabin and other party leaders signed a document at the beginning of April 1977 promising him that, in case of a peace agreement involving territorial concessions in the West Bank, the Government would call new elections.

FIRST MOVES OF THE CARTER ADMINISTRATION

The appointment of Professor Zbigniew Brzezinski as National Security Council (NSC) adviser, together with a number of statements by the new Secretary of State, Cyrus Vance, suggested that the Carter Administration's Middle East policy would closely follow the proposals of the Brookings Report. Vance's statement that "it is clear that the legitimate interests of the PLO must be dealt with"[18] was later described as a "slip of the tongue" in which he was referring to the previous formula used by the Ford Administration about the "legitimate rights of the Palestinians." However, Brzezinski went even further than Vance in his statement that a Palestinian state was "inevitable."[19]

The report of the Brookings Institution on the possibility of a ME settlement, published in December 1975, favoured a comprehensive agreement containing seven integrated elements:

1) **Security** All parties to the settlement should commit themselves to respect the sovereignty and territorial integrity of the others, and refrain from the threat or use of force against them.

2) **Stages** Withdrawal to agreed boundaries and the establishment of peaceful relations should be carried out in stages over a period of years, each stage being undertaken only when the agreed provisions of the previous stage have been faithfully implemented.

3) **Peaceful relations** The Arab parties should undertake not only to end such hostile actions against Israel as armed incursions, blockades, boycotts and propaganda attacks, but also give evidence of progress toward the development of normal international and regional political and economic relations.

4) **Boundaries** Israel should undertake to withdraw by agreed stages to the 5 June 1967 lines, with only such modifications as were mutually accepted. Boundaries would probably need to be safeguarded by demilitarized zones supervised by UN forces.

5) **Palestine** There should be provision for Palestinian self-determination, subject to Palestinian acceptance of the sovereignty and integrity of Israel within agreed boundaries. This might take the form either of an independent Palestine state accepting the obligations and commitments of the peace agreements, or of a Palestine entity voluntarily federated with Jordan but exercising extensive political autonomy.

6) **Jerusalem** The report suggested no specific solution for the particularly difficult problem of Jerusalem but recommended that, whatever the solution, it meet the following minimal criteria:

(a) there should be unimpeded access to all holy places, each under the custodianship of its own faith;
(b) there should be no barriers dividing the city;
(c) each national group within the city should, if it so desired, have substantial political autonomy within the area where it predominates.

7) **Guarantees** It would be desirable that the UN Security Council endorse the peace agreements. In addition, there might be a need for unilateral or multilateral guarantees to some or all of the parties, as well as substantial economic aid and military assistance, pending the adoption of agreed arms control measures.[20]

VANCE'S FIRST ME TOUR

The attempt to renew momentum towards a ME settlement began in mid-February 1977 with the US Secretary of State's seven-day visit to a number of capitals to obtain "at first hand" the Arab and the Israeli views on "how it may be possible to move forward to a peace settlement."

Opening his tour in Israel on 15 February, Vance's talks centred on the resumption of the Geneva conference and Israeli attitudes towards the PLO. Vance was told that Israel was prepared for the reconvening of the conference either "in its original format," or for any other framework "between the sovereign states of the area" with the aim of negotiating either "a comprehensive durable peace" or "the end of the state of war." Israel rejected any negotiations with the PLO, even if the organization recognized Israel or accepted Resolutions 242 and 338, but it did not oppose the participation of Palestinians in the Jordanian delegation to Geneva.[21] Vance and his aids apparently obtained the impression that Israel could change its attitude towards the PLO, if it recognized Israel.[22]

Vance told the Israelis that the Carter Administration accepted all the political commitments of its predecessor (as formulated in two published and one unpublished memoranda signed by the US and Israel on 1 September 1975[23] and in December 1973 respectively). These affirmed that Resolutions 242 and 338 were "the sole basis for any negotiations"; that "the composition of the participants of the Geneva conference" had to be determined "only with the consent of all parties concerned"; and that the US had "nothing to discuss with the PLO as a partner in the peacemaking process" as long as it refused to alter "the National Covenant" and did not accept Resolutions 242 and 338 (thus implying that the US attitude could change if the PLO changed its stand).[24]

Vance visited Cairo on 17–18 February after which Sādāt declared that there should be "a declared official relationship" between the Palestinian state and Jordan "even before the Geneva conference starts." This was understood to be a proposal to include the PLO in discussions, while indicating some compromise with the Israeli position; namely, that only Jordan was a valid partner in talks over the future of the West Bank.[25] Vance described this as "a constructive suggestion" which "begins to move" towards the Israeli stand. He said it showed that "more flexibility" existed in Egypt's position than he had thought. Israel's Foreign Minister, called it "a change in the right direction."[26]

Vance held talks in both Beirut and Amman on 18 February. Lebanese leaders said that their country would like to participate in the Geneva conference, but would not join the discussions on Israel's withdrawal since it had no border problems with Israel. Vance promised US support for Lebanon's participation. King Ḥusayn explained that he considered himself bound by the 1974 Rabat resolutions (that "the PLO was the sole legitimate representative of the Palestinian people" and had the right "to establish national authority . . . over any liberated

Palestinian territory.") He rejected a joint Jordanian-Palestinian delegation to Geneva unless the Rabat decisions were first revoked.[27]

In Riyadh on 19 February Saudi leaders asked Vance "to move towards recognition of the PLO in order to break the political logjam."[28] On 20 February, Vance held talks with the Syrian leaders in Damascus, who explained that in their view, there were three components to a settlement: 1) Israeli withdrawal from all the territories occupied in 1967; 2) recognition of the rights of the Palestinians; and 3) an end to the state of war.[29]

Vance's tour was summed up by the *Washington Post* as on the surface providing "little ground for optimism" about a settlement, since the parties delivered "unsurprising recitations of familiar and conflicting positions." However, there appeared to be "a real chance—far less than a probability but greater than a remote prospect—for a settlement," due to the new circumstances in the ME since the 1973 war and to the change in the US role in the area.[30]

RABIN'S VISIT TO WASHINGTON

The first ME leader to hold talks with Carter was Itzhak Rabin, who visited the US from 6–13 March. Carter's speech of welcome, on 7 March, seemed to come very close to Israeli positions. He spoke of his Administration's willingness "to explore some common ground so that Israel might have defensible borders, and so that peace commitments might never be violated. and so that there could be a sense of security about this young country in the future."[31] He defined peace as "the ending of the state of war, open borders, free movement of people and goods, and especially free exchange of ideas."[32] While Rabin was "pleased" with the statement on "defensible borders," it caused "some concern among experienced State Department officials" as well as Arab diplomats in Washington. Jody Powell, the White House Press Secretary hastened to explain that any interpretation of Carter's statement "should avoid a narrow definition of 'defensible borders' in geographic terms" because the President was speaking "in broad terms, reiterating the intent of the UN resolution about the 'secure' borders."[33]

Disclosures made after the elections in Israel revealed that in the private talks between Carter and Rabin, there had been sharp differences in attitude, aggravated by a lack of mutual sympathy between the two leaders. Carter was surprised at Rabin's categorical rejection of any negotiations with the PLO even if it recognized Israel, which stood in contrast to Vance's impression; he called it a "stiff and stubborn" attitude. He made it clear to Rabin that the US commitment not to recognize the PLO as long as the latter did not recognize Israel was still in force; but should the PLO change its attitude, the US would support its participation at Geneva. He emphasized his interest in a speedy reconvening of the Geneva conference, and said the US would not allow "procedural questions to prevent Israel's participation." If the PLO changed its attitude and Israel then decided to boycott the conference, Carter emphasized. "it will be a very serious problem" which "will provoke a very sharp reaction among the American people."

Regarding territorial problems, Rabin emphasized that Israel would not retreat to the 1967 lines, which Carter insisted upon. However, he asked Rabin whether Israel's distinction between "control" and "sovereignty" in the case of Sharm al-Shaykh could apply to other areas as well. Rabin replied that it "might be applicable in some areas," but that he had to consult his Cabinet. Despite Rabin's categorical rejection of the idea of "a third state between Israel and Jordan," Carter insisted upon the necessity of establishing some kind of a Palestinian entity. He also expressed American objection to new Israeli settlements in the occupied territories, saying he hoped that nothing would be done which would oblige the US to express this objection publicly.

In view of these differences, Rabin tried to obtain Carter's agreement not to commit himself to a new policy, or at least not to express it either in his forthcoming talks with Arab leaders or in public, because "any statement of the US . . . is equal to a precondition for the Geneva conference." However, he did not obtain such an assurance.[34]

Although Carter's 9 March statement (see immediately below), was felt by Rabin to be "a disappointing conclusion" to his talks,[35] he did not make public their difficult nature. He preferred to emphasize the "positive" results of his visit: 1) that the US would not enforce a solution; 2) that it was interested in a strong Israel; 3) that the American definition of peace had moved closer to Israel's; 4) that the US attitude towards the PLO had not changed; and 5) that "for the first time, we have heard from an American President support for the need of defensible borders and the possibility of distinguishing between defence lines and political borders."[36]

CARTER ON BORDERS AND A PALESTINIAN "HOMELAND"

At a press conference on 9 March (after Rabin had ended his official visit but was still in the US), Carter made a distinction between "permanent and recognized borders where sovereignty is legal"—the lines of which "I would guess . . . would be some minor adjustments in the 1967 borders"—and "defence lines," which might allow "extensions of Israeli defence capability beyond the permanent and recognized borders."[37]

This statement upset both Israel and the Arab states. Israeli sources expressed "deep disappointment" at its timing as well as over the "1967 borders concept." Rabin said that Israel "appreciates" America's understanding of the ME problem, but that eventually "it is up to the parties to the conflict to make final decisions," and that "when it comes to Israel's defence, Israel will decide what constitutes defensible borders—and not outsiders."[38] Sources in Cairo and Amman, as well as Arab diplomats in the US, expressed concern that Carter had apparently adopted the Allon Plan.[39] Official Arab reaction was more cautious. Sādāt said that "any talk about secure borders must take place within the framework of a comprehensive settlement," which included "the withdrawal of Israeli forces from all occupied Arab lands, respect for territorial integrity and non-acquisition of territories by force."[40]

In an attempt to influence the deliberations of the PNC, then in session in Cairo, Carter told a press conference on 16 March that "there has to be a homeland provided for the Palestinian refugees, who had suffered for many, many years."[41] 'Arafāt welcomed the statement, saying that Carter had "touched the core of the problem."[42] However, the next day a PNC spokesman, Maḥmūd Labadī, said that "even if that is 'Arafāt's opinion, we are not going to say we will not continue the struggle."[43]

Israel, though reacting cautiously, showed concern. Rabin said he "would have been happy if Carter had used a phrase other than 'homeland,'" adding that he would "have nothing against" Carter's statement if the President had meant that "the Palestinian homeland is in Jordan."[44] The Israeli embassy communicated Israel's immediate concern to the State Department, but US officials tried to diminish Carter's commitment; Brezezinski stated that the word "homeland" itself "has no specific connotation. The importance of the statement is in the broader approach it takes." However, on 19 March, Carter told correspondents that "what I said is appropriate. I think some provision has got to be made for the Palestinians in the framework of Jordan or by some other means."[45]

Jordan was also concerned by Carter's statement. Some ministers were reported to suspect that the US intended "to see a Palestinian state set up, not on the West Bank . . . as everyone supposed, but in Jordan itself." This suspicion was strengthened by the reports of CIA payments to Ḥusayn, and created a feeling among Jordanian leaders that a "plot" existed against the Kingdom.[46]

SĀDĀT'S VISIT TO WASHINGTON

Sādāt arrived in Washington for a three-day visit on 3 April 1977, after discussions in West Germany and France. At the welcoming ceremony, Sādāt lauded Carter's remarks about creating a "homeland for the Palestinian refugees," saying that Carter "came very close to the proper remedy." What was needed, he added, was to establish "a political entity, so that the Palestinians can at long last become a community of citizens, not a group of refugees."[47] According to the Egyptian ambassador to Washington, Ashraf Ghurbāl, the two Presidents agreed that "the Palestinians" would have "to be heard directly or by mediators," and that the only remaining question was how to achieve this.[48] However, according to a Lebanese newspaper, Sādāt did not succeed in convincing Carter to establish contacts with the PLO or to convene the Geneva conference with the participation of the PLO "at this stage."[49]

Another issue of disagreement between Carter and Sādāt was that of "defensible borders." Sādāt objected to any arrangement leaving Israeli or foreign defence installations on Arab territory since "sovereignty is indivisible, and there can't be two types of borders." He would agree only to demiltarized zones on both sides of the border on the Egyptian and Syrian fronts "on a reciprocal basis" and to "slight amendments" of the border in the West Bank in order to reunite divided villages—also "on a reciprocal basis."[50] Privately, however, Sādāt went further, and reportedly suggested that if Carter convinced Israel to withdraw, the US could use Sharm al-Shaykh as a naval base.

The third issue of disagreement was the "essence of peace." Here, too, Sādāt toned down his position and, according to US officials, told them that he envisaged a full normalization of relations with Israel within about five years after the Geneva agreement had been signed, and that some interim steps towards normal relations could take place even earlier.[51]

After his visit, Sādāt said in several interviews that five years after the peace agreement there would be a "normalization," but he declined to explain what he meant by this term and continued to reject diplomatic and commercial relations with Israel as well as other aspects of the Israeli-American definition of peace.

ELABORATION OF AMERICAN POLICY

Carter stated on 8 April that "there will have to be a spokesman for the [Palestinian] viewpoint during the [Geneva] conference itself" either "by a surrogate or by them directly."[52] He said on 22 April that he was trying "to learn the attitudes" of the Arab states and Israel, and "to observe and analyse some common ground on which a permanent settlement might be reached." Carter added that he intended "to minimize" his own statements until he had met all the leaders involved, since he had "outlined some of the options" and was "trying to get responses from them before I make further comments."[53]

ḤUSAYN'S VISIT TO WASHINGTON

King Ḥusayn arrived in Washington on 25 April and in an interview said he was "not optimistic about peace prospects in the ME this year."[54] The two-day talks centred on PLO representation in the Geneva conference, and on Carter's formula for "secure borders" and "a homeland for the Palestinians." Ḥusayn was reported to have objected to a joint Jordanian-PLO delegation and supported Asad's suggestion of a unified Arab delegation.[55] The White House press secretary subsequently reported that the US had not changed its "negative attitude" towards the PLO's participation in the Geneva conference, and that it objected to the inclusion of PLO representatives in the Jordanian delegation.

Husayn stated that Carter had assured him that in speaking of Palestinians, he had in mind only the West Bank and the Gaza Strip, whose status and relationship with Jordan should be defined later. Husayn's 1972 "Federation Plan" seemed to be one of the most probable solutions to this question.[56] Speaking in an interview with *CBS*, Husayn said it was "dangerous to speak about secure borders" in the ME, and emphasized that such borders could be possible only if the Arabs had a "true feeling" that they had got "a just and dignified solution [that] they are ready to live with and to observe."[57]

Carter said after his talks with the King that "it would be a mistake to hope for too much" because the differences between Israel and the Arab states were "very wide and have been lasting for a long period."[58]

"PERSUASIVE POWERS"

Carter announced on 2 May that he would not hesitate "to use the full strength of our own country and its persuasive powers to bring those [ME] nations to agreement" if he saw "a clearly fair and equitable solution." Although the US "cannot impose [its] will on others," it was in the position "of one who can influence countries to modify their positions slightly to accommodate other nations' interests." However, the President emphasized that "unless the countries involved agree, there is no way to make progress."[59]

Two days later, Vance stated that after completing the round of meetings with ME leaders, the US would be "prepared to make suggestions" about what it believed would be a "fair and equitable manner" of dealing with the ME problems, which it would then discuss with the parties concerned "to see how much common ground we can find." Answering a question whether these suggestions did not amount to a comprehensive plan, Vance said that whatever the name, it was "a question that gets into semantics." However, he also stressed that "the ultimate decision . . . must be made by the parties themselves."[60]

On several occasions, Brzezinski told American Jewish leaders that the election of a "weak" Israeli government would invite the US to impose a settlement.

THE ASAD-CARTER TALKS

Unlike other Arab leaders, Asad refused to visit Washington. His meeting with Carter was arranged (during Khaddām's Washington visit on 21–22 April) for 8–9 May in Geneva on "neutral ground"; it would fit between a seven-nation economic summit in London (7–8 May), a four-nation summit in Berlin (9 May) and a NATO Council meeting in London (10 May).

During the two-day talks, Asad reportedly told Carter that a "just peace" had to be based on UN resolutions and include both Israel's withdrawal from all the territories occupied in 1967 and recognition of the "legitimate rights of the Palestinians." He also expressed his belief that the US could and should impose such a settlement upon Israel. Carter answered that the US was preparing an "integrative plan" which could be a basis for the Geneva conference; this would be discussed by Vance during his second ME tour. Asad rejected the idea of "secure borders," but agreed to small demilitarized zones on both sides of the border. He insisted upon PLO participation in the Geneva conference within a unified Arab delegation and suggested (in the name of Syria, Egypt, Jordan, Saudi Arabia and the PLO) the establishment in the West Bank and the Gaza Strip of a Palestinian state linked with Jordan "in the same way some Arab states are linked to each other nowadays." [61]

Summing up the talks, Carter said "there must be a resolution of the Palestine problem and a homeland for the Palestinians . . . some resolution of border disputes and . . . an assurance of permanent and real peace with guarantees for the future security of these countries which all can trust." He added that all the ME leaders he met had agreed to the "general idea" of establishing buffer zones between Israel and her neighbours "manned by international peace forces," and that he agreed with Asad that these buffer zones had to be established on both sides of the border.

A senior US official told correspondents that there was optimism "that really serious negotiations will begin before the end of this year, even if not in the formal Geneva setting." [62]

HARDENING OF ARAB POSITIONS

The Arabs' "peace offensive" had been accompanied throughout by tough demands, such as for an Israeli ban on further Jewish immigration; but the frequency of their hardline statements increased from April 1977. Saudi and Egyptian officials hinted on several occasions that Resolution 242 should be changed to include the Palestinian people's problem; Saudi officials referred to the 1947 borders (established by the General Assembly Resolution 181) as the only legal Israeli borders, which a Syrian spokesman suggested Israel should draw back to. Sādāt said that he was "prepared to give six months"—no more—to Israel to withdraw from the occupied territories, and that he would claim $2,100m compensation from Israel for using the Sinai oilfields. Asad stated that recognition of Israel by Syria could not be a part of any settlement. [63]

ISRAEL'S CONCERN ABOUT AN IMPOSED SETTLEMENT

American statements produced growing concern in Israel, which made several unsuccessful diplomatic overtures after March 1977 to try to convince the US not to take "specific positions" over the terms of a political settlement, but to leave them, as promised, for negotiation between the parties involved. At a Cabinet meeting on 24 April, Allon reported that "the possibility of disagreement between Israel and the US over outstanding issues must not be ruled out." [64]

The cumulative impact of these various American statements and decisions created the impression among Israeli leaders that the US was beginning to exert pressure on Israel in order to force an American settlement in the ME. Among actions regarded as harmful to Israel's defence capabilities were the decision in February not to supply Israel with "concussion bombs" which had been promised by President Ford; the veto on Israel selling *Kfir* jets to Ecuador in March; and the proposal to exclude Israel from the preferred category of states receiving and jointly producing US weapons (put forward in Washington at the beginning of May). Israel's acting Prime Minister, Shimon Peres, declared that the US should offer its good offices to both sides, with a view to "building a bridge of understanding between their positions and smoothing the negotiating procedures," rather than putting forward its own proposals which could lead to confrontation "with either one side or both sides." [65]

THE ALLON-VANCE MEETING; FURTHER STATEMENT BY CARTER

Allon met Vance in London on 12 May to be informed officially of the results of

Carter's talks with Arab leaders. Afterwards, Vance announced that the US would act only as mediator and not initiate any peace plan of its own. He repeated the American commitment not to recognize or enter into direct contacts with the PLO "unless and until it accepts the UN resolutions and recognizes Israel's right to exist as a state." Vance also said that Carter's Administration fully endorsed the "special relationship" between the US and Israel, and that it would supply Israel "with all the arms it required for defence, including advanced technology."[66]

However, Israeli press reports spoke of continuing wide differences of opinion between Israel and the US regarding "defensible borders" and security arrangements, as well as over the problem of the "Palestinian homeland." Vance had also warned Allon that if Israel continued its policy of settlement in the occupied territories, the US would have to oppose it publicly, "which will be a pity."[67]

Carter said in Washington on 12 May that the first American commitment in the ME was "to protect the right of Israel to exist, to exist permanently, and to exist in peace." A part of this commitment was that "Israel had adequate means to protect itself without the military involvement of the US." On the other hand, Carter stated that if the PLO accepted the fact of Israel, Israel should agree to a homeland for the Palestinians. "The exact definition of what that homeland might be, the degree of independence of the Palestinian entity, its relationship with Jordan or perhaps Syria and others, the geographical boundaries of it, all have to be worked out by the parties involved." He added that he believed that "there is a chance that the Palestinians might make moves to recognize the right of Israel to exist, and if so, this would remove one of the major obstacles towards further progress."[68]

FAHD'S VISIT TO WASHINGTON

Prince (Amīr) Fahd of Saudi Arabia arrived in Washington on 24 May for a two-day visit—the first by an Arab leader since the election of the Likud government. His visit was preceded by a meeting between Sādāt, Asad and Saudi leaders in Riyadh on 19 May to co-ordinate their approach to the US.

Before leaving Riyadh, Fahd had said that Saudi Arabia could help to implement the "Carter plan" for energy conservation, but the US would have "to use her weight in order to achieve a just peace for the ME problem"; namely, "Israeli withdrawal from all the territories occupied in 1967" and the return "to the Palestinians [of] their rights in their homeland and to a state of their own."[69]

Carter subsequently denied that Fahd had explicitly linked Saudi oil policy with progress towards a ME settlement and that threats of a Saudi oil embargo had been made. Fahd was given to understand that the US had "some influence in Israel and also the Arab countries," but that it "obviously [has] no control over [them]."[70] However, in an interview, Fahd expressed his belief that the US, "which has a special military, political and economic relationship with Israel," could assist to achieve "a fair peace."[71] Carter said that Fahd had expressed "his strong hope that the Israelis would be reassured about the inclinations of his country towards the protection of their security."[72] This statement was interpreted by Israeli officials as support for Carter's idea about security arrangements beyond Israel's recognized borders.[73]

The main issue in the discussions between Fahd and Carter was the Palestinian question. Both sides were said to have agreed that the Palestinian problem was "still the main obstacle to resuming the Geneva conference," but they reached no agreement about PLO participation in it.[74] However after the talks, Carter said that "the Palestinians should have a secure homeland with recognized borders."[75]

REACTION TO THE ELECTIONS IN ISRAEL

Immediate Arab reaction to the unexpected victory of the Likud was one of surprise and concern about the prospects of a settlement. Arab media unanimously interpreted the victory by Begin (the "Zionist racist terrorist") as a blow to peace efforts, and as increasing the chances of war. Official comments, however, were more restrained. Ḥusayn said he was "concerned" about the election results, but "the positive and courageous stand" of the US was an "encouraging development."[76] Both Sādāt and the Jordanian Information Minister, 'Adnān Abū 'Awda, said that the results did not matter because "there is no difference between the Israeli leaders—all are hawks"; and because the real key to the settlement was in the hands of the US.[77]

While the US and other Western media expressed concern about the influence of the Likud's electoral victory on ME settlement prospects, the Administration's comments were restrained, emphasizing that "the historic friendship between the US and Israel was not dependent on the domestic politics of either nation,"[79] and that the US regarded itself committed to the "political process."[80]

THE WIDENING GAP BETWEEN THE US AND ISRAEL

After an assessment of the new situation, the Administration appeared to have decided to continue its policy and try to put pressure on the Begin government to moderate its attitudes—both in its official statements, and through the American Jewish community and the pro-Israeli lobby in Congress. This was strongly hinted at by Carter who said that the question of whether Begin would be an obstacle to the peace process "can be resolved . . . when he meets with the Congressional leaders and with Jewish Americans . . . I think this might have an effect on him."[81]

On 22 May, Carter stated that he expected "Israel and her neighbours to continue to be bound by UN Resolutions 242 and 338."[82] On 26 May, he repeated that the US was bound by the "premises" of a ME settlement, which had been "spelled out very clearly in UN resolutions . . . voted and supported by our Government." These resolutions included "the right of the Palestinians to have a homeland" and "to be compensated"; Israel's withdrawal from territories occupied in 1967; and "an end of belligerency and a re-establishment of permanent and secure borders."[83] Later on the same day, the State Department specified that the President "had in mind UN Resolutions 242 and 338," the "General Assembly Resolution 181 of November 1947 [which] provided for the recognition of a Jewish and an Arab state in Palestine, and the General Assembly Resolution 194 of December 1948 [which] endorsed the right of Palestinians to return to their homes or choose to be compensated."[84]

In the beginning of June, the President said that "if Israel should disavow those commitments [to UN resolutions made by former Israeli governments], that would be a very profound change," the consequences of which "cannot be accurately predicted."[85]

On 9 June, the US Assistant Secretary of State for Near Eastern and South Asian Affairs, Alfred L. Atherton, stated before the House of Representatives Subcommittee for International Affairs that if no settlement could be achieved, the US would have to reassess its aid to the ME "according to the policy of each country."[86]

On 17 June, Vice-President Mondale said that peace in the ME was essential for Israel. After reviewing Israel's achievements since its establishment, he added that regarding the future, "Israel's three million people" had either the choice to "try by force of arms alone to hold out against the hostility and growing power of the Arab world," or to start "a process of reconciliation" in which "peace protects Israel's security."[87]

The impression that the US and Israel were on a collision course reached a peak when the State Department stated on 27 June (i.e. after Prime Minister Begin had stated that everything, including the West Bank, was negotiable) that peace "requires both sides to make difficult compromises," and that "no territories, including the West Bank," can be "automatically excluded from negotiations." [88] A well-informed American correspondent quoted officials in Washington as having said that "if Begin cannot accept the idea of an Israeli withdrawal from the West Bank, there is no point in his coming next month to see President Carter." [89] Both this report and the statement itself caused embarrassment in Washington and Carter, who apparently had not been told about the latter, imposed a "moratorium" on statements about the ME.

The Carter Administration decided to avoid a public confrontation with Israel after failing to enlist American Jewish support, which instead had consolidated behind Israel. It was also faced with growing criticism from Congressmen and Jewish organizations, as well as mounting tension with Israel—where both the Government and the Opposition joined in criticizing recent American statements. In trying to improve the atmosphere for Begin's planned visit, Carter stated on 1 July that "an overwhelming consideration for us is the preservation of Israel as a free and independent and hopefully peaceful nation." He added that Begin "will be received with the kind of friendship that has always been characteristic of the American people's attitude toward Israel." [90] On 6 July, he assured American Jewish leaders that an overall ME settlement "would have to include diplomatic relations between the countries involved," and that the "Palestinian homeland or entity would have to have formal ties with Jordan." [91]

BEGIN'S FIRST MOVES

In view of the deep concern abroad about his victory and the sharp reaction to his first announcement (that the Allon Plan was dead, and that many settlements would be established in the West Bank), Menahem Begin began a campaign to change his negative image in the US. He gave numerous interviews with Western media and held meetings with US Congressmen and American-Jewish leaders who came to Israel to talk to the new Prime Minister. He also sent his adviser on foreign information, Shmuel Katz, to the US to explain the Likud's attitudes. Both Begin and Katz emphasized their desire for peace and their readiness to discuss any item raised by the Arabs. This campaign, as well as the appointment of Dayan as Foreign Minister and the erection of a coalition government at least partly succeeded in allaying US concern.

The Government programme stated, among other things, that it would honour all the commitments of the previous administration, including the acceptance of Resolutions 242 and 338 as the sole basis for a Geneva conference. It also confirmed that Israeli law would not be applied in the West Bank and the Gaza Strip, as long as negotiations with the Arab states continued.

After taking office, Begin set out to gain the political initiative from the Arab states. On 28 June, he suggested that the Geneva conference be reconvened at any date after 10 October 1977; and on 7 July, he suggested a "political truce" between Israel and the Arab states, to last until the Geneva conference was reconvened.

In mid-July, shortly before Begin's visit to Washington, the Israeli cabinet was reported to have approved a procedural plan for the Geneva conference to be submitted to Carter.

BEGIN'S VISIT TO WASHINGTON; PROCEDURAL PLAN REVEALED

Begin began his official two-day visit to Washington on 19 July, after meeting and receiving the backing of American-Jewish leaders in New York. The talks with Carter were termed "frank but friendly"; however, basic differences between the two leaders were not bridged. The Palestinian issue was discussed "primarily in a procedural context." The issue of Israeli settlements in the occupied territories was raised, and Carter emphasized American opposition to new settlements, but not to an "increase in the population" of existing ones. However, he did not obtain Begin's promise not to establish new settlements—even though he emphasized that he regarded this subject as a matter of mutual confidence. According to Israeli press reports, Begin did express readiness to make border changes in Sinai and the Golan Heights, but objected to any foreign control of the West Bank. Instead, he offered a version of the "Dayan Plan" according to which the residents themselves would manage the civil and administrative aspects of their lives, while Israel would be responsible for West Bank defence and security. However, he did not object to the placing of the West Bank on the agenda of the Geneva conference.

Unlike previous governments, Begin's strategy was to shift the burden of negotiation to contacts with the Arabs rather than with the US. Subsequently he did not try to reach a co-ordinated policy with Washington, and therefore differences did not immediately evolve into a dispute: both leaders "agreed not to agree." After the talks, both expressed optimism, and Carter said that they had "laid the groundwork" for reconvening the Geneva conference in October.[92]

At a press conference at the conclusion of his talks on 20 July, Begin revealed details of his procedural plan for the Geneva conference which he had submitted to Carter. The plan proposed the reconvening of the conference after 10 October on the basis of Resolution 338 (which refers to Resolution 242), with the participation of "delegations of sovereign states" only, and without "prior commitments" demanded or given. He further proposed that the delegations should form sub-commissions to negotiate and conclude bilateral "peace treaties," and that a full session of the conference should then be summoned to sign them. Begin stated that every peace treaty would include an opening article to the effect that "the state of war has been terminated," followed by territorial clauses, a chapter of diplomatic clauses, and finally economic and other clauses concerning specific problems. If the Geneva conference could not reconvene because of Arab insistence on PLO participation, Israel proposed either bilateral mixed committees with US chairmanship similar to the 1949 armistice negotiations in Rhodes, or "proximity talks" as suggested by the US in 1972.[93]

Carter termed the proposal "forward-looking and worthy of consideration."[94] The Arab leaders, however, rejected it categorically, especially since it completely ignored the Palestinian issue, and failed to ensure withdrawal from all the occupied territories. They also rejected the proposed alternatives for the Geneva conference.[95]

VANCE'S SECOND ME VISIT AND CARTER'S ASSESSMENT

The US Secretary of State's second ME visit took him to Alexandria (1–2 August), Beirut (3 August), Damascus (4–5 August), Amman (5–6 August), Tā'if (7–8 August), Jerusalem (9–10 August), and then back to Alexandria, Damascus and Amman (11 August), where he discussed questions of both procedure and substance and put forward American proposals.

With respect to procedure, Sādāt's suggestion that a "working group" of foreign ministers be convened in New York in September during the UN General Assembly (which had been accepted by both the US and Israel) was rejected by Syria. It was agreed, instead, to hold separate talks between the foreign ministers with Secretary Vance in New York.

According to press reports, Vance's substantive proposals included a phased five-year Israeli withdrawal linked to a gradual transition to full diplomatic relations; and an Israeli (or joint Israeli-Jordanian) trusteeship over the West Bank for several years, to be followed by a referendum to determine the area's future. These proposals were said to have been rejected by all the parties. The gap over the Palestinian and territorial issues also remained as wide as ever. However, on the "essence of peace," Egypt, Jordan and Syria were reported to be willing to sign peace treaties with Israel; while Egypt and Jordan were also ready "to consider" diplomatic relations.[96]

Dayan claimed that he had asked Vance to find out if the Arab states had any plans to solve the refugee problem after the peace treaty. Vance got negative answers. When reporting this in Jerusalem, a difference of opinion arose: Vance wanted to postpone dealing with the refugee problem, while Dayan argued that without a solution to it, there could be no final solution for the Arab-Israeli conflict.

After receiving Vance's report, Carter stated on 14 August that he remained determined "to do everything possible to bring about a just and lasting peace in the ME," and that he intended to meet the ME foreign ministers himself, in addition to their scheduled meetings with Vance. In an interview broadcast the same day, Carter said he would continue "to go public with the American position," adding: "I will feel much more secure when we take a strong position that I have the backing of the Congress and the American people." He went on to say that he was hopeful that "a final solution" could be reached, and that "world opinion is very powerful on disputing nations when there is a consensus about what ought to be done." He continued: "There is no single attitude among all Jews in the world or all Israeli citizens . . . [if] Israeli leaders genuinely want a peace settlement, . . . they have to agree that there will be an acceptance of genuine peace on the part of the Arabs, an adjustment of boundaries . . . which are secure for the Israelis and also satisfy the minimum requirements of the Arab neighbours and UN resolutions, and some solution to the question of the enormous numbers of Palestinian refugees who have been forced out of their homes and who want some fair treatment."[97]

On 29 August, Carter said that his Administration was "fervent" in its determination to make progress towards a ME peace "by the end of this year," and to that end "would be aggressive." He added that if there was no progress, "there is going to be a great deal of disillusionment on our part, in the ME and around the world." He said that the Arab leaders had exhibited a "more flexible attitude" than Israel during Vance's trip. Referring to the American media's description of the trip as a failure, Carter insisted that it was "very successful," and that there was still time for progress.[98]

THE BEGINNING OF US-ISRAELI CONFRONTATION

During August and the first half of September, two central issues became a matter of open controversy between the US and Israel: the former's attitude towards the PLO, and the latter's settlements in the West Bank.

Israel had decided to recognize three existing (but hitherto not officially recognized) settlements in the West Bank as "full-fledged settlements" on 26 July. On the same day, the State Department described Israeli settlement in the occupied territory as "illegal" and the decision as "an obstacle to peace." However, on 27 July, Carter said that it was not right to put all the blame on Begin because these and other settlements were "established under the previous government," and because Begin was bound by commitments made during the election campaign in the same way as Carter was bound.[99]

On 28 July, Carter for the first time expressed a US attitude which was interpreted by observers as a positive reference to the PLO. He stated that "the Palestinians" ought to be represented at the Geneva conference, and that the US would enter into discussions with them "at the time they forego their commitment to destroy Israel." [100]

On 8 August, following Vance's report from Tā'if that the PLO had conveyed to him its readiness to accept Resolution 242 if it was changed so as to include a recognition of Palestinian national rights, Carter stated that he would accept the Palestinians' recognition of "the applicability of UN Resolution 242" (tantamount to indirect recognition of Israel and its right to exist) as a sufficient condition for their participation in Geneva and for opening discussions with them. [101] This statement gave rise to speculation about an American or French initiative in the Security Council to change the resolution. However, both governments denied such an intention. Expectations of the PLO's qualified acceptance of Resolution 242 also remained unfulfilled; on 28 August, the PLO's Central Committee once again rejected it.

The shift in American attitude caused anxiety both in Jordan and in Israel. Jordan was also worried about a State Department statement that the US "has never recognized *de jure* the occupation of the West Bank by Jordan." Despite official denials by both Israel and Jordan, the press continued to report that Ḥusayn and Dayan had met in London during Dayan's visit (from 21–22 August) and had discussed the American attitude towards the PLO.

When Vance visited Jerusalem on 11 August, a delegation of West Bank personalities submitted a petition to him denying *inter alia* that the PLO was representative of the West Bank population. During August, several other West Bank leaders attacked the PLO and its leadership, a move apparently initiated by Jordan, with Israeli acquiescence. However, because it remained formally bound to the 1974 Rabat summit resolutions, Jordan welcomed the new American attitude. Dayan, on the other hand, termed the shift in attitude as a grave matter. He said on several occasions that if the US held talks with the PLO, it would violate the written American commitment given to Israel in 1975 in return for its withdrawal from Sinai. [102]

Presumably as a counter-move to this shift in Washington's position, Israel announced its decision to raise the standard of services provided by the government in the West Bank and Gaza Strip to that in Israel. Three days later, on 17 August, Israel announced its decision to establish three new settlements in the West Bank. The US again described the establishment of settlements as "illegal" and "obstacles to peace," but tried to play down their importance; it denied that the two countries were on a collision course. The State Department changed the sentence which had originally described the decision about equal services as "an action which could only complicate the peace process" to read: "The Israeli government has emphasized the potential benefit to the population in the occupied territories of the humanitarian aims of this action." [103] Carter stated he did not intend "to go further" than the "open expression of our own concern and the identification of these settlements as being illegal." [104]

On 9 September, the Minister of Agriculture and Chairman of the Joint Government-Jewish Agency Committee for Settlement, Ariel Sharon, said in an interview that "new settlements have been set up in [Judea and Samaria] which have not been reported." [105] Because the widespread criticism evoked by the statement, Sharon hastened to deny charges that new settlements were secretly established, and said he had been misunderstood; [106] the US expressed its satisfaction with the Israeli denial. [107] In view of the forthcoming meetings of the foreign ministers and the fact that Israel refrained from any new activities in this matter, the issue of Israeli settlements in the West Bank receded for the time being, while the more important questions of Palestinian representation in Geneva and the solution of the Palestinian problem remained at the forefront of political activity and public interest.

Israel's longstanding policy of rejecting PLO (or any other independent Palestinian delegation's) participation in Geneva received overwhelming affirmation in a Knesset resolution adopted in September, which stated that the PLO "is not a discussion partner for the State of Israel in any ME peace negotiations."[108] Instead, Israel insisted on the primacy of making peace with "sovereign states." Accordingly, the Government prepared a draft of a peace proposal which was presented by Dayan to Carter at a meeting on 19 September. Little attention was paid to it by the Americans, and after Fahmī's rejection (at his meeting with Carter on 21 September), the draft proposal was abandoned. Begin also rejected Asad's suggestion that the Arab League should represent the Palestinians,[110] provided there were guarantees that the "rights of the Palestinians" would be discussed at the conference.[111]

The US, on the other hand, emphasized the centrality of the Palestinian issue. In an interview published on 9 September, Carter described the PLO's rejection of Resolution 242 as "an obstacle in the way of our efforts to convene a peace conference," and expressed the hope that the organization would "re-examine its position on this matter." Reiterating his views on the requirements of a settlement, the President warned that if "either Israel or the Arabs cling to their very adamant positions of the past and refuse to negotiate freely and aggressively, then there is no hope for a permanent peace." In such a case, he added, "it will be difficult for us to continue to devote that much time and energy to the ME. Dozens of other foreign policy matters require my urgent attention."[112] On 12 September, the US issued a statement declaring that "to be lasting, a peace agreement must be positively supported by all the parties to the conflict, including the Palestinians. This means that the Palestinians must be involved in the peacemaking process. Their representatives will have to be at Geneva for the Palestinian question to be solved."[113] On 18 September, a day before Carter's meeting with Dayan, the American ambassador to the UN, Andrew Young, stated that the PLO should be represented in the Geneva conference, because in its absence no peace treaty could be signed. However, the White House spokesman declined to comment on this.[114]

THE POINT OF US-ISRAELI CONFRONTATION

In the expectation of an approaching confrontation between the United States and Israel, attention became focused on the meetings of the Americans with Dayan rather than with the Arab foreign ministers. The two main issues at Dayan's first meeting with Carter, Mondale and Vance on 19 September were Palestinian representation at Geneva and the Israeli settlements. Carter emphasized that the Palestinians must be represented.[115] According to Israeli press reports, the President suggested that a unified Arab delegation would be the best solution to the problem. Dayan rejected this idea, saying that Israel wanted to negotiate with "sovereign states" and that she had already agreed to the participation of Palestinians in the Jordanian delegation. However, US officials thought that Dayan's answer left the door open for further consideration. Dayan also rejected any negotiations with the PLO as such, but told the Americans that Israel would not reject the participation of PLO sympathizers within the Jordanian delegation, so long as they did not publicly declare their support for the PLO. He expressed Israel's readiness to negotiate with a Palestinian delegation outside the framework of the Geneva conference and on condition that the negotiations were not aimed at establishing a

Palestinian state.[116] On 22 September, Dayan and Vance arrived at a compromise formula, which was approved by the Israeli government on 25 September. The formula, which according to Begin was approved "word for word,"[117] called for a unified Arab delegation in which "Palestinians who are not known members of the 'PLO' may participate . . . as a part of the Jordanian delegation." This unified delegation would take part *only* in the opening ceremony, and then "split up into delegations representing the various states" to conduct bilateral negotiations.[118]

Egypt, Jordan and Syria rejected the proposed formula outright as an "Israeli manoeuvre" to foil the Geneva conference, and emphasized that "there will be no Geneva without the PLO."[119] The US expressed its satisfaction with Israel's acceptance, but emphasized that "some of the conditions set by the Israeli cabinet yesterday do not accurately reflect our views," such as the reference to the PLO. Vance told reporters that "Israel has not gone far enough to help to resolve the continuing procedural stalemate."[120]

During the following week, the US tried to extract further concessions. The Americans were reported to have urged Israel to modify its position and agree to the participation in Geneva of second-rank PLO officials, as well as to an independent Palestinian delegation within the unified Arab delegation. Dayan and other Israeli spokesmen persistently repeated Israel's categorical rejection both of PLO participation in Geneva and of an independent Palestinian delegation—because in both cases it would signify that the creation of an independent Palestinian state was on the agenda. Accordingly, Dayan warned that the implementation of either alternative would destroy the chances for the reconvening of the Geneva conference.

These attempts to pressure Israel prompted a great deal of criticism within the US. On 20 September, Senator Richard Stone, chairman of the sub-committee for the ME and Europe, declared his support for the Israeli draft proposal and accused the Administration of not abiding by its commitments to Israel. On 28 September, two US Senators separately accused the Administration of urging Iran "to threaten to curtail its oil supplies to Israel as a means of putting pressure on Israel to make concessions in the ME negotiations."[121] The State Department's denial of these charges did not diminish criticism of the Administration's policy. In a last effort to break the deadlock, a meeting between Carter and Dayan was arranged for 5 October. But before the meeting took place, an event occurred which brought to a head not only the confrontation between Israel and the US, but also the criticism within the US of the Administration's policy.

THE AMERICAN-SOVIET JOINT COMMUNIQUÉ

On 1 October, Vance and the Soviet Foreign Minister, Andrei Gromyko, issued a joint communiqué which stated that "as soon as possible a just and lasting settlement of the Arab-Israeli conflict" should be achieved. The key issues for such a settlement were "withdrawal of Israeli armed forces from territories occupied in the 1967 conflict; the resolution of the Palestinian question including ensuring the legitimate rights of the Palestinian people; termination of the state of war and establishment of normal peaceful relations on the basis of mutual recognition of the principles of sovereignty, territorial integrity and political independence." This settlement should be achieved through the reconvention of the Geneva conference "not later than December 1977, with the participation in its work of the representatives of all the parties involved in the conflict, including those of the Palestinian people, and legal and contractual formalization of the decisions reached at the conference."[122]

The joint communiqué aroused widespread criticism against the Carter Administration inside the US and in Israel, based on four principles. 1) Failure to mention Resolutions 242 and 338 as the basis for the negotiations, and a peace treaty as their aim. 2) The term "legitimate rights" was interpreted as acceptance both of the PLO as a legitimate negotiating party, and of the idea of a Palestinian state. 3) The American-Soviet statement was interpreted as tending to undo US efforts to restrict Soviet influence in the area by presenting the Russians with an opportunity to regain a prominent position in any future Arab-Israeli negotiations. 4) It implied an imposed solution.

In his address to the UN General Assembly on 4 October, Carter seemed to be trying to mollify both Israel and his American critics. He stated that "true peace—peace embodied in binding treaties—is essential"; that it was crucial for Israel to have "borders that are recognized and secure" as well as "security arrangements"; and that "the commitment of the US to Israel's security is unquestionable." He emphasized that Resolutions 242 and 338 were "the basis for peace," and that there must be "a recognition by all nations in the area—Israel and the Arab countries—[that all the parties] have a right to exist in peace, with early establishment of economic and cultural exchange and normal diplomatic relations." However, the President also held that "the legitimate rights of the Palestinian people must be recognized . . . How these rights are to be defined," he added, "is, of course, for the interested parties to decide in negotiations and not for us to dictate." [123]

THE AMERICANS AND DAYAN AGREE ON A "WORKING PAPER"

At that juncture, the prospects of Dayan's 5 October meeting with Carter and Vance seemed dim indeed. According to Israeli sources, Dayan termed the discussion "brutal." Carter accused Israel of being obstinate and therefore an obstacle to the peace process—"even more than Syria." He urged Israel to agree to the participation of second-rank PLO officials in Geneva, and warned that if Israel continued to be an obstacle, he would address the American public and explain that Israel was hurting American interests. Carter explained that he was well aware that in such a case he would have to face strong opposition in the US, but he would present Israel's supporters with the alternative of supporting either Israeli or American intersts.

Dayan stated in no uncertain terms Israel's objections to, and fears of, a Palestinian state or even an entity. With regard to Carter's promise of a US commitment to Israel's security, Dayan said that Israel would not like to count on the US for defence, even if she could be sure that the US would honour its commitments. But in this regard the American record was poor. Dayan recalled a number of instances in the past when US Presidents had, in Israeli opinion, acted in a way prejudicial to vital Jewish interests. These included Roosevelt's refusal in 1943 to save Jews by bombing German extermination camps; Truman's embargo on arms supplies in 1948; and Johnson's unwillingness to implement Eisenhower's promises of 1957 when Nāsir closed the Tiran straits in 1967. [124] However, at the end of their two-hour discussion, Carter and Dayan arrived at a compromise formula the details of which were then worked out between Vance and Dayan and set forth in what has come to be known as the "Working Paper". Its text was as follows:

1. The Arab parties will be represented by a unified Arab delegation, which will include Palestinian Arabs. After the opening sessions, the conference will split into working groups.

2. The working groups for the negotiation and conclusion of peace treaties will be formed as follows:

a. Egypt-Israel

b. Jordan-Israel
c. Syria-Israel
d. Lebanon-Israel [if and when Lebanon requests to join the conference]

3. The West Bank and Gaza issues will be discussed in a working group to consist of Israel, Jordan, Egypt and the Palestinian Arabs.

4. The solution of the problem of the Arab refugees and of the Jewish refugees will be discussed in accordance with terms to be agreed upon.

5. The agreed basis for the negotiations at the Geneva Peace Conference on the Middle East are UN Security Council Resolutions 242 and 338.

6. All the initial terms of reference of the Geneva Peace Conference remain in force, except as may be agreed by the parties.''[125]

In the joint communiqué, announcing this Working Paper, the US and Israel stated that ''all understandings and agreements between them on this subject remain in force,'' and that ''acceptance of the joint US-USSR statement of 1 October 1977 by the parties is not a prerequisite for the reconvening and conduct of the Geneva conference.''[126] On 12 October, the Israeli government approved the Working Paper as a basis for reconvening the Geneva conference, but made it clear that no further concession would be made. The main achievement of the Paper was to avert a full-scale American-Israeli confrontation. However, the many questions that stood in the way of reconvening the Geneva conference remained unresolved.

The stalemate following the September talks and the US-Israeli Working Paper continued until 9 November 1977, when Sādāt's offer to address the Knesset initiated his visit to Jerusalem (19–21 November) and changed the situation dramatically (see essay on ''The Middle East in Perspective'').

NOTES

1. *Al-Jumhūriyya*, Cairo; 3 November 1976.
2. Sādāt in an interview with *Time*, New York; 29 November 1976.
3. Middle East News Agency (MENA), 9 November—Daily Report (DR), 10 November 1976. Similarly, MENA, 14 and 17 November 1976.
4. Interview with *Le Monde*, Paris; 21 January—DR, 28 January 1977.
5. *New York Times* (*NYT*), 1 December 1976.
6. *NYT*, 13 January 1977.
7. Interview with *Time*, 29 November 1976.
8. *Die Arbeiter-Zeitung*, Vienna; 13 February 1977.
9. MENA, 20 March—BBC Summary of World Broadcasts (BBC), 22 March 1977.
10. *Ha'aretz* and *Ma'ariv*, Tel Aviv; 28 November 1976.
11. Interview with *Newsweek*, New York; 14 January 1977.
12. Interview with *Washington Post* (*WP*), 29 December 1976.
13. Interview with National Broadcasting Corporation (NBC), quoted by MENA, 3 January—DR, 4 January 1977.
14. R Cairo, 14 January 1977.
15. The joint communiqué as transmitted by R Cairo and R Amman, 15 January—BBC, 17 January 1977.
16. Interview with *The Sunday Telegraph*, London; 16 January 1977.
17. Interview with *Time*, 24 January 1977.
18. At the Senate Foreign Relations Committee hearing on 11 January 1977. Quoted by *NYT*, 12 January 1977.
19. *Ma'ariv*, 4 and 5 February 1977.
20. *Towards Peace in the Middle East: Report by a Study Group* (Washington: The Brookings Institution, 1975), pp. 1- 2.
21. Allon addressing a dinner party in honour of Vance, Israel Government Press Office, *Daily News Bulletin* (GPO/D), 16 February 1977. Similarly, in Allon's replies to two motions for the agenda in the Knesset; *Ma'ariv* and *Jerusalem Post* (*JP*), 16 February 1977.
22. *Ma'ariv*, 3 June 1977.

23. For texts, see *NYT*, 17 and 18 September 1975.
24. Israeli Cabinet communiqué; GPO/D, 20 February 1977. *Ha'aretz*, 17 and 18 February 1977. *The Dept of State Bulletin* (*DSB*), Washington; 21 March 1977, p. 249. *NYT; International Herald Tribune* (*IHT*), Paris; And *Christian Science Monitor* (*CSM*), Boston; 17 February 1977.
25. MENA, R Cairo, 17 February—DR, 18 February 1977. *NYT, Baltimore Sun*, 18 February 1977.
26. *NYT, IHT*, 19 February 1977. Israeli Broadcasting Authority (IBA), 20 February—DR, 28 February 1977.
27. MENA, 19 February 1977. For text of the Rabat decisions, see R Cairo, Voice of the Arabs (VoA), 29 October—BBC, 20 October 1977.
28. *Ma'ariv*, 20 February 1977.
29. R Damascus, 20 February—DR, 21 February 1977.
30. *WP*, 23 February 1977.
31. *NYT, IHT, Ha'aretz*, 8 March; *DSB*, 4 April 1977, pp. 310–11.
32. *Weekly Compilation of Presidential Documents*, 14 March 1977, p. 323.
33. *NYT, IHT*, 8 March 1977.
34. Rabin in an interview with *Ma'ariv*, 15 July; and in an article in *Yedi'ot Aḥaronot*, Tel Aviv; 5 August. Begin in a statement in the Knesset on 27 July, 31 August—*Ma'ariv*, 28 July, 1 September. *Ha'aretz*, 17 March, 23 August. *Ma'ariv*, 3 and 10 June 1977.
35. *Ha'aretz*, 10 March 1977.
36. GPO/D, 13 March 1977.
37. *DSB*, 4 April 1977, p. 306.
38. In a speech before the Congress of Presidents of Major Jewish American Organizations on 9 March—*JP*, 10 March 1977.
39. *CSM*, 10 March; *Ma'ariv*, 11 March 1977.
40. In an interview with American Broadcasting Corporation (ABC) screened on 13 March—*JP*, 14 March 1977.
41. *DSB*, 11 April 1977, p. 385.
42. *The Guardian*, London; 18 March 1977.
43. *Arab Report and Record* (*ARR*) *1977*, London; p. 229.
44. *JP*, 18 March 1977.
45. *JP*, 20 March 1977.
46. *The Times*, London; 3 April; *Ha'aretz*, 22 March 1977.
47. *DSB*, 2 May 1977, pp. 434–6. *IHT, Guardian*, 5 April 1977.
48. Interview with *al-Musawwar*, Cairo; 29 April 1977.
49. *Al-Dustūr*, Paris; 18 April 1977.
50. Sādāt in interviews with Walter Cronkite (CBS) and Barbara Walters (ABC) and in a press conference on 6 April, quoted by MENA, 6 and 7 April—DR, 7 April. R Cairo, 6 April—DR, 12 April 1977. *Al-Dustūr*, 18 April 1977. For Sādāt's alleged remark concerning Sharm al-Shaykh, see *Arabia and the Gulf*, London; 2 May 1977.
51. *NYT*, 9 April 1977.
52. *DSB*, 9 May 1977, p. 461.
53. *DSB*, 16 May 1977, p. 481.
54. Interview with CBS, quoted by *JP*, 25 April 1977.
55. MENA, 27 April 1977. *Ha'aretz*, 26 and 27 April 1977. *Ma'ariv*, 27 April 1977.
56. Husayn in a press conference on 26 April, quoted by MENA, 27 April 1977. *NYT, Ha'aretz*, 27 April 1977.
57. R Amman, 30 April 1977.
58. *Ma'ariv*, 27 April 1977.
59. *DSB*, 30 May 1977, p. 547.
60. *DSB*, 23 May 1977, pp. 516–17.
61. R Damascus, 8–10 May; *al-Nahār*, Beirut; 10 and 13 May; *Ma'ariv*, 9 and 10 May 1977. The quotation from *al-Nahār*, 13 May 1977.
62. R Damascus, 10 May; *NYT, Ma'ariv*, 10 May 1977.
63. Sādāt, in an interview with *Rastakhiz*, as published by MENA, 18 May—DR, 19 May; R Cairo, MENA, 29 May—DR, 31 May 1977. Asad, in an interview with Danish journalists, R Damascus, 14 June—DR, 15 June 1977.
64. *Ha'aretz, Ma'ariv*, 25 April 1977.
65. *JP*, 9 May 1977.
66. *The Guardian*, 13 May 1977.
67. *Ma'ariv*, 16 May, 3 and 10 June 1977.
68. *NYT*, 13 May 1977.
69. MENA, 21 May 1977.
70. United States Information Service (USIS), *News Report*, 26 May 1977.

71. *Newsweek*, 6 June 1977.
72. Carter after the talks, quoted in USIS, *Official Text*, 26 May 1977.
73. *Ma'ariv*, 29 May 1977.
74. Deutsche Presse Agentur (DPA), 25 May 1977.
75. *JP*, 25 May 1977.
76. Interview with *NYT*, 1 June 1977.
77. MENA, 20 May—BBC, 23 May 1977.
79. White House spokesman's statement on 18 May, quoted by *Ha'aretz*, 19 May 1977.
80. State Department statement, quoted by *Ha'aretz*, 19 May 1977.
81. *NYT*, 27 May 1977.
82. *NYT*, 23 May 1977.
83. In a press conference transcribed by *NYT*, 27 May 1977.
84. Official text of the statement.
85. Interview with *US News and World Report*, Washington; 6 June 1977.
86. *Ma'ariv*, 9 June 1977.
87. In his speech before World Affairs Council of Northern California in San Francisco, transcribed by USIS, *Official Text*, 20 June 1977.
88. USIS, *News Report*, 28 June 1977.
89. Quoted by *JP*, *Ha'aretz*, 28 June 1977.
90. *IHT*, 2-3 July 1977.
91. *JP*, 7 July 1977.
92. USIS, *Official Text*, 20, 21, 25 July; GPO/D, 25 July 1977.
93. Official transcript of the press conference.
94. USIS, *News Report*, 20 July. Similarly, USIS, *Official Text*, 13 July 1977.
95. E.g. see interviews of Asad and Ḥusayn with *Newsweek*, 1 August 1977.
96. *NYT, IHT*, 22 August 1977.
97. USIS, *News Report*, 16 August 1977.
98. USIS, *Official Text*, 30 August 1977.
99. USIS, 26 July; USIS, *Official Text*, 28 July 1977.
100. USIS, *Official Text*, 29 July 1977.
101. USIS, *Official Text*, 9 August 1977.
102. E.g. see an interview with *Ma'ariv*, 19 August 1977.
103. USIS, *News Report*, 19 August; *Ma'ariv*, 19 August 1977.
104. USIS, *Official Text*, 24 August 1977.
105. *Ma'ariv*, 9 September 1977.
106. GPO/D, 10 September 1977.
107. *NYT*, 10 September 1977.
108. *JP*, 2 September 1977.
109. Interview broadcast over the IDF Radio, 6 September—DR, 7 September 1977.
110. *JP*, 31 August 1977.
111. Interview with *NYT*, 29 August 1977.
112. *JP, Jewish Chronicle*, London; *al-Nahār*, 9 September 1977.
113. *IHT*, 13 September 1977.
114. USIS, 22 September 1977.
115. USIS, *News Report*, 20 September 1977.
116. *Ma'ariv*, 20, 21 September 1977.
117. IBA, 29 September—BBC, 1 October 1977.
118. GPO/D, 25 September; IBA, 25 September—DR, 26 September 1977.
119. Fahmī as quoted by MENA, 26 September and *WP*, 27 September. For the Jordanian and Syrian reactions, see R Amman and R Damascus, 25 September—BBC, 27 September 1977.
120. *The Times, WP*, 27 September 1977.
121. *NYT*, 29 September 1977.
122. USIS, *Official Text*, 3 October 1977.
123. USIS, *Official Text*, 5 October 1977.
124. *Ma'ariv, Yedi'ot Aḥaronot*, 21 October 1977.
125. GPO/D, 13 October 1977.
126. USIS, *News Release*, 5 October 1977.